BIBLE READING

Study Guide

——❊——

A Basic Bible Study

Your Bible reading guide to people,
places, and happenings from the Creation
in Genesis to the Four Horsemen in Revelation

S. E. M^CEVERS

ELECTRIC
MOON
PUBLISHING

BIBLE READING
Study Guide

A Basic Bible Study

**Learn about people, places, and happenings from the
Creation account in Genesis to the Four Horsemen in Revelation.**

Dear Bible Reader,

If you have ever been interested in what the Holy Bible has to say, but have hesitated reading it because it seemed a daunting task, this study guide may be just what you are looking for. It will be your personal tutor to keep you on track as you read this all-time bestseller.

This study guide is designed with simple chapter outlines followed by questions about people, places, and happenings that will keep your interest. References are provided to help locate the answers.

It will not teach you the Bible. Instead, you will discover for yourself what it has to say by reading each small chapter and answering a question or two. It will not discuss doctrine, teach theology, or get involved in denominational differences. It is designed to simply provide you with a fundamental knowledge of the Bible.

There might be passages that you do not understand. That is to be expected. However, as you work your way through the lessons at your own pace, you will quickly realize how easy it is to gain a basic understanding of the Bible.

This Bible study guide was designed for individual use, but can easily be used for a group study. Although it is best to start with lesson one and work your way through the lessons chronologically, it is possible to go directly to a particular book and study it.

This study guide workbook can be used with the online study guide found at www.simple biblelessonsforyou.com.

The online site contains links to extra information to take your reading to a higher level.

Your mentor,

S. E. McEvers

CONTENTS

GENESIS
The Beginning of Time

Genesis covers about 2000 years from Creation to Joseph, the great-grandson of Abraham, the patriarch of the Jewish people. Adam and Eve's choice affected history forever. Cain murdered his brother, all people turned from God except Noah, who escaped the flood. After the flood, Abraham's descendants became the Hebrew nation.

Ch. 1–2 Creation

Ch. 3 Temptation, Verse fifteen is the first promise of a redeemer. He would restore what was lost.

Ch. 4 Cain and Abel

Ch. 5 Adam's family

Ch. 6–8 Flood, Giants mentioned (see Numbers 13:33; 1 Chronicles 20:4–8)

Ch. 9 The Rainbow (9:13–16) God's Symbol

Noah probably knew the grandson of Adam. Noah's father probably knew Adam's son. After the flood, Noah lived long enough to know Abraham.

Ch. 10 Noah's descendants

Ch. 11 Tower of Babel

Ch. 12 Abram is called to follow Him, and the lineage of the Hebrew people begins.

Ch. 13 Abram and Lot go separate ways—Lot's choice? Abram's attitude?

Ch. 14–18 Son is promised (Compare 18:14 with Luke 1:37 and Jeremiah 32:17)

Ch. 19 Sodom and Gomorrah

Ch. 20 Abraham lies

Ch. 21–24 Isaac

Ch. 25–31 Jacob has 12 sons who became the 12 tribal leaders of the nation of Israel

Ch. 32–36 Jacob's name changed to Israel; Jacob and Esau's family and relationship

Ch. 37–39 Joseph is sold into slavery; Judah's sin.

Ch. 40–50 Joseph becomes second-in-command in Egypt and can provide for his family during a famine. His family—father, all his brothers and their families—moved to Egypt, 66 people in all. With Joseph, his wife, and two sons the whole of Jacob's family in Egypt was 70 people.

PEOPLE, PLACES, HAPPENINGS

Who were there at the beginning? (1:26; 3:22; John 1:1–3; Colossians 1:16)

Who were to rule the animals? (1:28)

If there was no rain until the flood, how was the vegetation watered? (2:6)

How did God make the woman? (2:21–24)

How did the serpent begin his temptation? What were his first four words? (3:1)

What did he tell Eve? (3:4–5)

Did it end well? (3:7–24)

How is it that all people are sinners? (Romans 5:12, 17, 19)

How old was the oldest person, and who was he? (5:27)

Did Noah have to round up the animals? (6:20)

Where did all the flood waters come from? (7:11)

What did the rainbow symbolize? (9:13–17)

How old were Abram and Sarah when God spoke to Abram about his descendants? (12:4; 17:17)

What was God's prophecy concerning Abram's offspring? (15:13–14)

How old were Abraham and Sarah when God spoke to Abraham again about a son? (17:1, 17)

How did God respond when Sarah laughed at the thought of having a baby? (18:12–15)

How many sons did Isaac have? (25:24)

How many sons did Jacob have? What were their names? (Ch. 29–30; 35:18, 23–26)

Why did Joseph's brothers hate him? (37:4)

How did Joseph prosper as a slave? (39:2, 21; 41:37, 39)

What brought Joseph's brothers to Egypt? (41:55—42:3)

What brought Jacob/Israel to Egypt? (45:1–28)

How old was Joseph when he died? (50:22)

A NOTE FROM YOUR BIBLE STUDY MENTOR

You have made it through the first book of the Bible. A lot of history is covered in that first book. Now we come to Exodus. This tells the story of the Hebrews in Egypt, their mistreatment, and their freedom from slavery.

How are you doing so far? Good? I hope so. There is so much to discover in this journey through the Bible. Keep up the study. *Hint:* When you sit down to study, look at the next question and read to find that answer. That will make this more like a treasure hunt.

EXODUS
Exodus from Egypt

At the end of Genesis, Israel and his family had moved to Egypt seeking relief from a famine. That family stayed and grew to 2–3 million people. In Genesis 15, God promised Abraham he would be the father of a great nation, and they would have their own land. Now four centuries later, it was time. A Hebrew boy, Moses, miraculously survived babyhood to become God's chosen, but reluctant, leader for his people.

Ch. 1 Hebrew population grew; Egyptian ruler was concerned

Ch. 2–3 Moses called (3:14; Hebrews 11:23–29)

Ch. 4–11 His dealings with the Pharaoh

Ch. 12 Passover (see Hebrews 9:12, 14, 22, 24, 26; 10:1, 4, 14)

Ch. 13–18 Journey out of Egypt begins, God provides for them

Ch. 19 God met them at Mt. Sinai (19:5, 12, 18)

Ch. 20 Ten Commandments (see Romans 3:23) no one could keep all the law

Ch. 21–31 Various laws and procedures

Ch. 32 People turned to worship something they made (see Acts 7:17–41)

Ch. 33–34 Moses' relationship with God (see Psalm 145:8–9)

Ch. 35–40 Tabernacle and furnishings

PEOPLE, PLACES, HAPPENINGS

How old was Moses when he saw the mistreatment of the Hebrew slaves and killed one of the slave masters? (Acts 7:22–24)

How many years passed from the time he ran away to Midian and tended sheep to the time when God called him from the burning bush? (Acts 7:29–30)

What did God call Himself? (3:14)

How many plagues were there? List them. (Chapters 7–11)

What was the final plague? (Ch. 11)

What were the Hebrews to do to protect their families from the death of their firstborn? (12:7)

Who was to see the blood? (12:13)

Was the ground dry when the Hebrews crossed the Red Sea or was the water shallow? (14:21–22)

What happened when the Egyptian army tried to follow them? (14:24–28)

How did God provide for their nourishment? (16:9–16)

What was the complaint of the crowd of Israelites? (17:1–3)

What did Moses do? (17:4)

How did God provide for them? (17:5–6)

What are the ten commandments? (20:3, 4, 7, 8, 12, 13, 14, 15, 16, 17) Briefly list them.

How many times were the men to present themselves before God each year? (23:17)

How did Moses respond to God's anger at the people? (32:7–13)

If God refused to forgive the people, what would Moses request? (32:32)

What did the people do each time Moses went into the tabernacle? (33:7–11)

How did God talk with Moses? (33:11)

Who stayed in the tabernacle longer than Moses? (33:11)

What set these people apart from all other people? (33:15–16)

What part of God was Moses allowed to see? (33:23)

How did God describe Himself? (34:6–7)

When Moses came down from the mountain, what did he look like? (34:29–35)

Where did the supplies come from for the building of the tabernacle and its furnishings? (35:5–29; 11:1–3; 12:35–36)

What guided the people on their journey? (40:34–38)

A NOTE FROM YOUR BIBLE STUDY MENTOR

You have made it through the first two books. Great! Do you feel good about knowing more than when you first started this journey? You can do this!

The next book will be Leviticus, which can be a dry book, but it does have some treasures. I will guide you through it. I find it interesting that God provided laws that would protect His people from the spread of disease. Also, there is a lot of typology in this book. The sacrifices, the feasts, and the tabernacle all have meanings that foretell the Messiah.

LEVITICUS
Laws

God gave laws which would set them apart from other nations. The laws taught them reverence, protected them from spreading diseases, and governed their nation. The Day of Atonement reminded them of the Passover and pointed to a future, final atonement.

Ch. 1–7 Requirements for offerings—Damaged or second–rate offerings were not allowed. Only the best. Offerings for various occasions.

Ch. 8–9 Dedication of Aaron and sons—Great care was taken to prepare them for their priestly duties.

Ch. 10 Profane worship (see Exodus 30:9; Numbers 3:1–4)

Ch. 11 Dietary rules—It appears that what they could not eat, at least in part, were scavengers and bottom feeders.

Ch. 12 Childbirth rules

Ch. 13–15 Leprosy and other physical maladies

Ch. 16 Day of Atonement (Compare with Hebrews 7:27; Hebrews 9–10; Isaiah 53:6) Most important day of their year.

Ch. 17 Eating blood

Ch. 18 Sexual morality

Ch. 19–20 Other rules and penalties

Ch. 21–22 Rules for priests, purity

Ch. 23 The seven yearly feasts

Ch. 24 Care of the Tabernacle

Ch. 25 Poor, and slaves, slavery was common practice

Ch. 26 Blessings (26:1–13); curses (26:14–46)

Ch. 27 Redeeming pledges

PEOPLE, PLACES, HAPPENINGS

Who were Aaron's sons? (1:5; see Exodus 28:1)

What kind of offering could they bring? (1:3)

After offering a small portion of the grain offering, what was the rest for? (2:3, 10)

What part of the sacrifice were they never allowed to eat? (3:14–17)

What happened when the anointed priest sinned? (4:3)

What could they bring for a trespass offering? (5:6–11)

What were the rules for keeping the fire on the altar? (6:12–13)

What did the priests receive of the offerings for their food? (7:29–36)

Where were Aaron and his sons to remain for seven days after their dedication? (8:35)

How did the people know God approved the priestly ministry and offerings? (9:23–24)

Why did two priests die? (10:1–7)

How was God to be regarded by those who came near to Him? (10:3) What does regard mean?

What could not be eaten? (Ch. 11)

Why do you think there were dietary rules?

Would following rules prevent diseases? (11:24–40)

Why follow the rules? (11:45)

How could the priest tell if a sore was leprosy? (13:3)

How often was the Day of Atonement? (16:29–33)

Why was this day so important? (16:34)

What was the final Day of Atonement? Hebrews (9:23–28)

Why were they to obey God's sexual morality laws? (18:1–5, 24–30)

What would happen to a parent who gave their child as a sacrifice to Molech? (20:2)

Why did the priests have such strict laws to live by? (21:6)

Why were there strict laws regarding sacrifices? (22:32)

List the seven yearly feasts. Were there other special days? (Ch. 23)

Although slavery was common around the world at that time, how were God's people to be different? (25:39–55)

A NOTE FROM YOUR BIBLE STUDY MENTOR

You have made it through Leviticus. That is more than most people can say, even church–going people. What did you learn about God? His expectations? His provisions?

The fourth book of the Old Testament is Numbers. It tells of the journeys of the Hebrew people as they wandered for forty years before going into the promised land. What kind of organization must it have taken to move so many people?

When they set up camp, there was a plan. It was not haphazard. It needed to be very well organized, or there would be chaos.

NUMBERS
Wandering

The Israelites prepared to follow God into the promised land. However, when they saw the difficulties ahead, their unbelief in God's provision stopped their progress. Forty years they wandered in the wilderness before the next generation was allowed to move into the promised land.

Ch. 1–2 Census of the tribes except for the Levites

Ch. 3–4 Census of the Levites and their duties (Hebrews 4:14—5:11)

Ch. 5–8 Other laws and procedures

Ch. 9 Second Passover

Ch. 10 Organization of tribes

Ch. 11 People complain, and God's provision

Ch. 12 Dissension of Aaron and Miriam—Moses' siblings

Ch. 13 Spies sent in and bring back a report of unbelief

Ch. 14 People refuse to enter, results, (14:11–19) Moses intercedes

Ch. 15 Laws, pardon for sin, presumptuous sin (arrogantly, revolt)

Ch. 16 Rebellion against Moses with the support of the people; God wanted to teach them that this was a theocracy, not a democracy

Ch. 17–18 Aaron's position, priestly duties (Hebrews 7:5)

Ch. 19 Laws

Ch. 20 Moses' disrespect of God, Aaron dies

Ch. 21 Bronze serpent

Ch. 22 Talking donkey

Ch. 23–24 Balaam's prophecies

Ch. 25 People sin

Ch. 26 Second Census

Ch. 27 Joshua chosen to lead

Ch. 28–30 Various laws

Ch. 31 War with Midianites

Ch. 32 Tribes settling east of Jordan

Ch. 33 Journey reviewed

Ch. 34–36 Land division

PEOPLE, PLACES, HAPPENINGS

Who were counted in the census? (1:1–47) Who were not counted? About how many people were there altogether?

Of the Levi family of Gershon, how many were there and what were their duties? (3:21–26)

Of the Levi family of Kohath, how many were there and what were their duties? (3:27, 31)

Of the Levi family of Merari, how many were there and what were their duties? (3:33–37)

To serve in the tabernacle, how old did a Levite male need to be? (4:3, 23, 30, 35)

What was the total number of Levites that were of serving age? (4:36, 40, 44, 48)

Who received two carts and oxen, and who received four carts and oxen? (7:6–9)

What guided them during the day? What guided them during the night? (Ch. 9)

Describe the frustration Moses felt with the complaining people? (11:11–15)

How did God help Moses? (11:16–17)

What happened to Miriam for complaining against Moses? (12:10)

How many spies went to Canaan? (Ch. 13)

Did they all come back with a bad report? (Ch. 13)

What was Israel's sin? (14:11; Compare with Hebrews 3 and 4)

What was Moses concerned about in his prayer for the people? (14:13–19)

Why were there tassels on the priest's garments? (15:37–41)

What did the budding of Aaron's rod solve? (17:1–11)

How did Moses disrespect God? What was the consequence? (20:1–12)

What caused the plague in chapter 21, and what brought an end to it?

Compare this story with John 3:14–15. How would Jesus die?

How many times did Balaam hit his donkey? (22:28)

What did the donkey see that Balaam didn't see? (22:31)

What was the census at the end of these years of wandering? (26:51)

Was it more or less than at the beginning?

Would any lamb do for sacrifice? (28:19)

A NOTE FROM YOUR BIBLE STUDY MENTOR

You have completed the first four books of the Old Testament. Have you surprised yourself to get so far?

Deuteronomy, the next book, is a book of remembering. In today's world, we have special days and ceremonies to remind us of certain important events lest we forget and make the same mistakes.

This book has the same purpose—to remind the Hebrew people who they are, who God is, and who they are without Him. "Remember," says Moses, "lest you forget."

Understanding the God of the Old Testament will help us comprehend His mercy shown in the New Testament.

Are you ready to study, Deuteronomy, the fifth book in the Old Testament? There is much treasure in this book. At the completion of this lesson, you will have read and studied the entire Pentateuch, the first five books of the Old Testament. Awesome!

DEUTERONOMY
Remembering Lest They Forget

Remembering is the theme of the book of Deuteronomy. Moses admonished the people to remember God and what He had done for them. His disrespect for God kept him from entering the promised land. Joshua was appointed as their new leader.

Ch. 1 Moses is speaking to the people after 40 years of desert travels immediately before they were to complete their journey and enter the land of promise.

Ch. 2–3 Because of God's presence with them, the other countries would be afraid of them (2:25)

Ch. 4 If they would believe, God's presence would be with them. Other nations would take notice; no one like God (4:15–40)

Ch. 5 Review of ten commandments

Ch. 6 Greatest Commandment (see Matthew 22:37)

Ch. 7 Special people because God chose them

Ch. 8 When they come to the place when they say they don't need God (see Jeremiah 2:31)

Ch. 9 More remembrances

Ch. 10 Essence of law

Ch. 11–13 Serious relationship with God

Ch. 14–19 Review of laws

Ch. 20 Warfare

Ch. 21 Laws concerning murder, and other problems

Ch. 22–25 Review more laws, moral and sanitation

Ch. 26 Requirements for offerings, regular provision for the poor

Ch. 27–29 Blessings for obedience; Cursings for disobedience

Ch. 30 Blessing for returning to God;

Ch. 31 God's promise to go with them

Ch. 32 Moses' song

Ch. 33 Final blessing

Ch. 34 Moses dies

Note—Word or phrases that were repeated: 4:4 hold fast; 4:6 be careful; 4:9 lest you forget;

PEOPLE, PLACES, HAPPENINGS

Why was God angry with them? (1:32–33)

Which two of the spies would be able to go into the promised land? (1:36–38)

How big was King Og's bed? (3:11)—a cubit is about 18 inches

He warned them to take heed, lest they did what? (4:9, 23)

What is the greatest commandment? (6:1–5; specifically v. 5)

Why did God choose them? (7:8; Compare with John 15:16)

How is God described in 10:17–21?

What did God set before them? (11:26)

Could they offer second–rate or blemished animals for sacrifice? (17:1)

What customs were they to avoid in their new land? (18:9–14)

Who was this Prophet mentioned in 18:15? (see Acts 3:18–26)

What were they to do with runaway slaves? (23:15–16)

If they made a loan, could they charge interest? (23:19–20)

What proclamation was made in chapter 26? (26:17)

What did God proclaim? (26:18–19)

List five curses, if they didn't obey. (27:11–26)

List five blessings, if they obeyed. (28:1–14)

He told them that they would perish if they did what? (30:17–18)

He called heaven and earth as witnesses as He told them what? (30:19–20)

Who was inaugurated to lead them after Moses died? (31:14, 23)

Why could Moses not go into the promised land? (32:48–52; see Numbers 20:1–12)

Who buried Moses? (34:5–6)

A NOTE FROM YOUR BIBLE STUDY MENTOR

Congratulations on making it through the first five books of the Old Testament (Pentateuch). You have done well and are on your way to having a basic understanding of the Bible. A foundation has been laid. The following lessons will build on that foundation. The next several books are categorized as historical books.

Joshua, now 85 years old, is the leader of this new nation. He guides them for another 25 years as they conquer and settle the land. How well will they do?

What was Joshua's formula for success?

Keep going strong. This book is full of fascinating history.

JOSHUA
Settling the New Land

LESSON

6

Joshua is the first of the historical books. As their new leader, he was responsible for leading the Israelites into the land God promised and dividing it among the twelve tribes. After their first victory at Jericho, they were soundly defeated at Ai. Through that loss, they learned that God was to be respected. The people worshiped and obeyed God as long as Joshua lived.

Ch. 1 God speaks to Joshua

Ch. 2 Rahab

Ch. 3 God's presence, symbolized by the ark, was to go before them as they crossed the Jordan River.

Ch. 4 Crossing Jordan, setting up a memorial at Gilgal, a place of remembrance

Ch. 5 The people prepare to take the land (see Exodus 16 and Numbers 11)

Ch. 6 Destruction of Jericho

Ch. 7 Defeat at Ai; Joshua was concerned for God's reputation (7:8–9)

Ch. 8 Victory at Ai

Ch. 9 Deceit of the Gibeonites

Ch. 10 Sun stands still (see 2 Kings 20:11)

Ch. 11–19 Conquering land and division of land

Ch. 20 Cities of refuge

Ch. 21 Levites' inheritance

Ch. 22 Altar by the Jordan

Ch. 23 Joshua's final speech

Ch. 24 Choices

PEOPLE, PLACES, HAPPENINGS

What was to be Joshua's key to a successful life? (1:7–8)

37

Why did Rahab hide the spies? (2:9–13)

What were the stones to memorialize? (4:7)

Why the memorial? (4:22–24)

When did God cease from providing manna? (5:10–12)

How many days did they march once around the city? (6:3, 11, 14)

How many times did they march around the city on the seventh day? (6:15)

Why did they suffer defeat at Ai? (7:10–11)

How did Joshua and the people carry out the command of Moses in Deuteronomy 27? (8:30–35)

How did the Gibeonites deceive Joshua? (9:1–15)

Why were Joshua and the leaders deceived? (9:14)

Why did the Gibeonites deceive Joshua and the leaders? (9:24)

Were they allowed to live? (9:26)

What happened to them? (9:27)

What killed more of their enemies? The sword or hailstones? (10:11)

About how long did the sun stand still? (10:13)

Why did Caleb get Hebron for an inheritance? (14:14)

List the first five tribes that received their allotted land. (13:15—17:18)

List the next tribes that received their allotted land. (18:11—19:48)

What were cities of refuge for? (20:1–9)

If the Levites didn't get any land, what did they get for their inheritance? (21:1–2)

Why did they build the altar at the Jordan River? (22:26–29)

What did Joshua want the people to decide? (24:14–18)

Did the people keep their word? (24:31)

A NOTE FROM YOUR BIBLE STUDY MENTOR

You are doing great! What do you think about the Hebrew people by now? Has it turned out well for them?

After Joshua dies, the people are led by a series of judges for over three hundred years. There is no central government at this time as recorded in the book of Judges.

You will read about how the people repeatedly wandered away from God, got into trouble, and were rescued when they repented and called out to God. When they prayed, God appointed a judge to lead them out of trouble.

One of the judges was a woman named Deborah.

JUDGES/RUTH
Quickly Wandering Away from God

After Joshua died, there was no central government and no strong spiritual leadership. The next generation did not know God and repeatedly drifted into idol worship. God allowed enemies to invade causing the people to pray. He appointed judges to govern them.

Ch. 1 Incomplete conquest of the new land

Ch. 2 Joshua dies

Ch. 3 Three judges (compare 3:5–6 with Deuteronomy 7:3–6)

Ch. 4–5 Female judge; God gives them victory over their enemy

Ch. 6 Insignificant Gideon is called to lead

Ch. 7 Gideon's mighty army of 300

Ch. 8 Gideon and his army subdue their enemy

Ch. 9 Abimelech becomes king through treachery

Ch. 10 Israel harassed on both sides by enemies

Ch. 11–12 Jephthah, son of a mistress, becomes a leader

Ch. 13 Samson's birth

Ch. 14–16 Samson gives into the duplicity of a beautiful woman

Ch. 17–21 A time of no judges

PEOPLE, PLACES, HAPPENINGS

How long did the people serve God? (Joshua 24:31; Judges 2:7)

What happened after Joshua died? (2:11–17)

What did God provide for them? (2:16)

How did history repeat itself over and over again? (2:16–19)

Who were the three judges listed in chapter 3?

Why were the foreigners left in the land? (3:4)

Who did Barak insist go with him in war? (4:8)

Who was the judge in chapters 6–8?

What was God's opinion of Gideon? (6:12)

What was Gideon's opinion of himself? (6:15)

God trimmed the army from _____ to _____ to deliver the people. (7:1–7)

As soon as Gideon was dead, what did the people do? (8:33–35)

How did Abimelech die? (9:53)

What was Jephthah's vow to God? (11:30–31)

What wonderful thing did the Lord do when Manoah and his wife made their offering? (13:19–20)

What was the symbol of Samson's strength? (16:17)

How many times did he trick Delilah? (Ch. 16)

Who stole his mother's silver? (17:2)

When the silver was returned to her, what did she do with some of it? (17:4)

Why was there a battle between 11 tribes of Israel and their brother tribe of Benjamin? (20:1–48)

How did the Israelites live during this time period? (21:25; 17:6)

RUTH
Redemption

Ch. 1 Ruth and Naomi return to Judah

Ch. 2 Ruth gleans in the fields for food

Ch. 3 Naomi gives Ruth instructions for meeting Boaz

Ch. 4 Redemption

PEOPLE, PLACES, HAPPENINGS

Why did Elimelech and Naomi move to Moab? (1:1–2)

Of their family, who returned to Judah? (1:7, 14, 19)

Who returned to Judah with Naomi? (1:16)

What did Ruth give up by going back with Naomi? (1:15–17)

Would she ever go back to her country? (1:17)

What did Boaz do to marry Ruth? (Ch. 4)

How was she related to King David? (4:21–22)

A NOTE FROM YOUR BIBLE STUDY MENTOR

After years of being led by judges, their culture is about to change. As a result of a woman's desperate prayer, a boy is born and becomes a judge. Samuel, the last judge, is their leader until God appoints a new king through Samuel at the request of the people.

Now they have a strong central government, at least, for a while. What do you think of their insisting on having a king?

In this book, 1 Samuel, you will learn about the conflict between Saul and David and learn about the character of both men.

1 SAMUEL
Reign of Saul

After 350 years of feeling different, the people wanted to be like the nations around them. God told Samuel, the prophet, to anoint Saul to be their first king. Shortly into his reign, he lost the anointing because he disrespected God. Jealous of David, Saul became a madman driven to take David's life. Eventually, Saul and his sons were killed in battle.

Ch. 1 Hannah's despair, prayer, and joy

Ch. 2 God reprimands Eli for allowing his sons' corrupt behavior

Ch. 3 Samuel's first prophecy

Ch. 4 Ark captured; the ark represented God's presence

Ch. 5 The Ark of God versus Dagon

Ch. 6 The Ark sent back in a cart pulled by milk cows

Ch. 7 Samuel becomes judge and conquers the Philistines

Ch. 8 Israel wants a king like the nations around them

Ch. 9–12 Saul chosen to be king (note 10:17–24)

Ch. 13 Saul's unlawful sacrifice,

Ch. 14 Jonathan and David become best friends

Ch. 15 Saul rejected as king (Compare verse 22 with Psalm 51:17 and Isaiah 57:15)

Ch. 16 Young David anointed to be king

Ch. 17 David vs. Goliath Because of his experiences as a shepherd, David had become very acquainted with his God and knew Him well. He was convinced the God he knew would help him destroy that arrogant boaster.

Ch. 18 Saul is jealous and angry with David

Ch. 19 Compare with Psalm 59

Ch. 20 Jonathan's loyalty, not to his crazy dad, but to his innocent best friend, David. Note—In our culture kissing is reserved for romance and older female relatives kissing young children. In the Middle East and other cultures, it has always been expected that people of both genders to kiss on both cheeks when greeting a friend or family member, and kiss to say goodbye. Farewells could be very emotional. (see Genesis 29:13)

Ch. 21 Compare with Psalm 56

Ch. 22 Compare with Psalm 52

Ch. 23 Compare with Psalm 31, 54

Ch. 24 David does not want to retaliate against Saul (see Psalm 57)

Ch. 25 Samuel dies, David prevented from killing out of anger

Ch. 26–27 Again David does not harm Saul when he has an opportunity

Ch. 28–30 War

Ch. 31 Saul and sons die

PEOPLE, PLACES, HAPPENINGS

Why was Hannah so sad? (1:2)

How did Eli misinterpret Hannah's praying? (1:13)

How did Hannah express her gratitude to the Lord for giving her a son? (1:28, 2:11)

What did Eli do wrong? (2:29)

Describe Samuel's experience. (3:1–9)

What was the prophecy? (3:10–14)

Compare 3:19–20 with Deuteronomy 18:20–22. What makes a true prophet?

How did Eli die? (4:18)

What happened to the god of the Philistines when placed by the ark? (5:1–4)

What happened to the Philistines when the ark was in their territory? (5:6)

How did the Philistines know the illnesses they had were because of the ark? (5:6–12)

How long was the ark in Kirjath Jearim? (7:2)

What does "Ebenezer" mean? (7:12)

Who did Israel reject? (8:7)

Who was chosen to be king? (9:15–17; 10:1, 6, 24)

What did he look like? (9:2; 10:23)

Was it wrong to ask for a king? (12:19)

Why was Saul's sacrifice wrong? (13:8–13)

What quality was God looking for in a man to be king? (13:14)

What was Saul's excuse for disobeying God? (15:24)

Why did Samuel anoint David to be the future king? (16:1)

What service did David provide for Saul? (16:14–23)

How tall was Goliath? (17:4)—a cubit is about 18 inches

How did David know that God would deliver him? (17:37)

Why was Saul angry with David? (18:8–12)

What did Saul do when he was angry with David? (18:11; 19:10)

What did Saul do when he was angry with Jonathan? (20:33)

How did David disguise himself before Achish? (21:12–15)

Who became David's followers, and how many were there? (22:1–2)

Why did David not kill Saul? (24:6)

How was Saul's life spared again? (26:7–23)

What was Saul's sin in chapter 28? (Compare with Deuteronomy 18:9–14).

A NOTE FROM YOUR BIBLE STUDY MENTOR

You've done well. Let's keep going and find out more about this imperfect king, David, the man God said was after His own heart. David becomes king during difficult circumstances. Through his mistakes, he shows us that repentance is essential.

As the study of Israelite history continues, two books, 2 Samuel and 1 Chronicles, will be combined as their stories overlap. Although they can be read separately, it is best to read them together.

2 SAMUEL/1 CHRONICLES
King David

This lesson combines 2 Samuel with 1 Chronicles as those accounts overlap. For seven years, not everyone supported David, the new king. This godly king was not perfect. He sinned and tried to hide it by committing another sin. When confronted by the prophet Nathan, King David admitted his guilt and prayed for God's forgiveness. His life was characterized by humility. ***NOTE:*** The first nine chapters of First Chronicles are the genealogies of the twelve tribes of Israel starting with Adam and ending with the reign of David.

2 Samuel	1 Chronicles
Ch. 1 David respects God's anointed (see Psalm 18)	1 Chronicles 10
Ch. 2 David anointed king of Judah; reigns in Hebron	
Ch. 3 Civil War	
Ch. 4 War ends	
Ch. 5 David reigns over combined Israel and Judah, 33 years	1 Chronicles 11, 12, 14
Ch. 6 Bringing Ark to Jerusalem is treacherous	1 Chronicles 13–16
Ch. 7 David wants to build God a temple; God says no	1 Chronicles 17
Ch. 8 Victories (see Psalm 60)	1 Chronicles 18
Ch. 9 Remembering his friend, Jonathan	
Ch. 10 More victories	1 Chronicles 19
Ch. 11 David's major sin	
Ch. 12 Prophet Nathan confronts David; (see Psalms 25, 51) Solomon, the future and wisest king is born	1 Chronicles 20
Ch. 13 Rape, murder	
Ch. 14 Absalom returns	
Ch. 15 Treason David's reign depends on God's wishes; he does not defend himself (15:25, 26; see Psalm 3)	
Ch. 16 David and supporters on the run (16:9–12) David does not retaliate but waits on God. He only wants God's will even if it meant he was dethroned.	
Ch. 17 More running	
Ch. 18 Absalom dies	

2 Samuel	**1 Chronicles**
Ch. 19 David's return to Jerusalem; He does not seek revenge (16:5–12; 19:18–23)	
Ch. 20 Cessation?	
Ch. 21 Reparation to Gibeonites, Philistines destroyed, remaining giants killed (see 1 Samuel 17; Deuteronomy 3)	
Ch. 22 David composes a song of praise (see Psalm 18)	
Ch. 23 Recollection of David's war heroes	
Ch. 24 David's census and consequences	1 Chronicles 21–29

PEOPLE, PLACES, HAPPENINGS

How long did David reign over Judah while in Hebron? (2:1–3, 11)

Who was crowned king of Israel? (2:8–9)

Who was Mephibosheth's father? Why was David concerned about him? (Ch. 4)

How old was David when he began to reign? (5:4)

How long did David reign in Jerusalem? (5:5)

How long was the ark in the house of Obed–Edom? (6:11)

What was David's attitude when he went before God? (7:18–24)

Why did he want to know if any of Saul's descendants were alive? (9:1)

What was David's sin? (Ch. 11)

How did he try to cover it up? (Ch. 11)

Was he found out? (Ch. 12)

Who confronted David and how? (12:1–15)

What happened to the baby? (12:15–19)

What was the name of Bathsheba and David's second son? (12:24–25)

What was Amnon's sin? (Ch. 13)

What did Absalom do to Amnon? (13:23–33)

How long did Absalom hide out in Geshar? (13:38)

Why did David have to flee the city? (15:14)

Who cursed David and threw rocks at him? (16:5–13)

What was David's reaction? (16:10–12)

Was Hushai loyal to Absalom? (17:5, 14, 15, 16)

How did David react to the news of Absalom's death? (18:33; 19:1–8)

Did David seek revenge against Shimei? (19:18–23)

How many giants were killed? (21:15–22)

Why did David feel guilty? (24:10)

A NOTE FROM YOUR BIBLE STUDY MENTOR

David is nearing the end of his life. In the next lesson, 1 Kings/ 2 Chronicles, who will become king? Will he be a godly king? Will the country be strong? Who will be king after him? Will he be godly? Clue: conflicts will arise in the royal family.

What do you think? Do they have a peaceful country? Why or why not?

Keep up the good work. Step by step, question by question, you will make it through this entire course. Right now, concentrate only on the next question. You are doing well!

1 KINGS/2 CHRONICLES
Judah and Israel Split

The books of 1 Kings and 2 Chronicles cover the same history from different points of view. David's son Solomon followed him as the next king of Israel. God blessed him with wisdom and wealth. 1 Kings 8 shows his humility during his early reign. By chapter 11, his focus was not on God but on women and wealth. In 931 B.C., the kingdom split into Israel and Judah.

1 Kings	2 Chronicles
Ch. 1–2 David dies, and Solomon becomes king	1 Chronicles 28–29
Ch. 3–4 Solomon prays after a dream	2 Chronicles 1
Ch. 5–7 Solomon builds temple	2 Chronicles 2–4
Ch. 8 Prayers of dedication and ark is brought in	2 Chronicles 5–7
Ch. 9–11 Solomon's achievements	2 Chronicles 8–9
Ch. 12–14 The kingdom splits	2 Chronicles 10–12
Ch. 15–16 Kings of Israel	2 Chronicles 13–18
	Kings of Judah
Ch. 17 Elijah the prophet comes on the scene	
Ch. 18 Elijah proves who is the real God	
Ch. 19–22 King Ahab, evil king; Jehoshaphat	2 Chronicles 19–20
reigns in Jerusalem	2 Chronicles 21
Jehoram	

PEOPLE, PLACES, HAPPENINGS

What did Solomon ask God for in chapter 3? (1 Kings 3:5–9)

What else did God give him? (1 Kings 3:13–14)

How great was Solomon's wisdom? (1 Kings 4:29–31, 34)

Why did Solomon request lumber from Hiram, king of Tyre? (1 Kings 5:6)

Compare 1 Kings 8:27 with Jeremiah 23:24 and Isaiah 66:1. How are they similar?

After sinning, what was to be the process of restoration? (1 Kings Ch. 8)

Why did Solomon ask God to hear the foreigner's prayers? (1 Kings 8:43; 2 Chronicles 6:33)

Compare 1 Kings 8:46 with Romans 3:23 Who sins?

Who was he talking about in 2 Chronicles 7:14?

What was so important in 1 Kings 8:57–61?

Compare 1 Kings 8 with 2 Chronicles 6–7. What does Solomon ask God for when the people return to God after they sin?

Why did the queen of Sheba visit Solomon? (1 Kings 10:1–7)

Compare 1 Kings 11:4 with Deuteronomy 7:3, 4. What warning did God give the people through Moses?

Why did the kingdom split? (1 Kings 11:11–13)

Did Rehoboam listen to his father's advisors? (1 Kings 12:6–8)

Why did all the Levites move into Judah? (2 Chronicles 11:14–17)

Why did disaster come to Jeroboam? (1 Kings 14:7–10)

What did God promise Asa? (2 Chronicles 15:2)

What was Hanani's message to Asa? (2 Chronicles 16:7–10)

Who was God looking to help? (2 Chronicles 16:9)

How did Elijah prove who was the real God? (1 Kings 18:20–40)

How many times did Elijah's servant look for rain before he saw a small cloud? (1 Kings 18:41–46)

Did God reveal Himself in the wind, fire, or earthquake? (1 Kings 19:11–12)

How did God show Himself to Elijah? (1 Kings 19:12)

What kind of ruler was Ahab? (1 Kings 21:25–26)

Why did Ahab hate Micaiah? (1 Kings 22:8; Compare with Isaiah 30:1–14)

How did Ahab die? (1 Kings 22:29–40)

Why was God with Jehoshaphat? (2 Chronicles 17:3–4)

How did he improve the spiritual condition of his country? (2 Chronicles 17:6–9)

Did Ahaziah follow in his father's footsteps? (1 Kings 22:52)

How were the judges to judge? (2 Chronicles 19:7, 9)

When Jehoshaphat was faced with an invasion, what did he do? (2 Chronicles 20:3, 12)

Did he win? (2 Chronicles 20:27)

A NOTE FROM YOUR BIBLE STUDY MENTOR

In the next lesson, you will read about some miracles like the law of gravity being suspended, a jar of oil that doesn't run dry, and a man that goes directly to heaven without dying.

At the end of this lesson, you learned about King Ahab's death. What will happen to his evil queen? Find out in the next lesson, 2 Kings/ 2 Chronicles.

2 KINGS/2 CHRONICLES
Who Will Heal Their Backsliding?

From the time of Solomon's death, Israel did not listen to God's prophets. Eventually, Judah followed Israel's spiritual downfall. Godly rulers tried to restore the worship of God, but it was quickly undone by ungodly rulers. Prophets delivered messages from God, but the majority of the people did not want God.

2 Kings	2 Chronicles
Ch. 1 King Ahaziah looks to Baal–Zebub instead of the Lord God	2 Chronicles 22
Ch. 2 Last days of the ministry of Elijah; Elisha takes his place	
Ch. 3 Moab against Israel	
Ch. 4 Miracles	
Ch. 5 Naaman	
Ch. 6 War and famine	
Ch. 7–8 Victory over King Ben–Hadad and the Syrians	
Ch. 9–10 Jehu is king and rids the country of all of Ahab's sons; Jezebel dies	
Ch. 11 Athaliah kills all heirs so she can reign, but Joash is hidden until there is a coup and he is anointed king	2 Chronicles 23
Ch. 12 Joash reigns and makes great improvement in the temple	2 Chronicles 24
Ch. 13 Prophet Elisha dies	
Ch. 14 Amaziah reigns in Israel	2 Chronicles 25
(Other prophets during this time were: Jonah, Amos, Hosea.)	

PEOPLE, PLACES, HAPPENINGS

What did the Lord tell Elijah to prophesy against Ahaziah? (2 Kings 1:3–4)

How did Elijah respond to the fifty men sent to escort him to the king? (2 Kings 1:10)

What happened the third time the king sent men to Elijah? (2 Kings 1:13–15)

What did Elisha want? (2 Kings 2:9)

What was required of Elisha to receive his wish? (2 Kings 2:10)

How did Elijah leave this life? (2 Kings 2:11)

How did God provide for a widow? (2 Kings 4:1–7)

Did laying the staff on the face of the dead child revive him? (2 Kings 4:31)

How was he revived? (2 Kings 4:33–35)

Who was Naaman? (2 Kings 5:1)

Why was Naaman angry? (2 Kings 5:11–12)

What was Elisha's response to his servant's fear at seeing the great enemy army? (2 Kings 6:16–17)

Why was the city deserted? (2 Kings 7:6–7)

What was left of Jezebel to bury? (2 Kings 9:35)

Was she buried? (2 Kings 9:36–37)

How long did Ahaziah reign? (2 Chronicles 22:1–2)

Who advised Ahaziah to do wickedly? (2 Chronicles 22:3)

Why was Joash hidden and for how long? (2 Chronicles 22:10–12)

Describe Athaliah. (2 Kings 11; 2 Chronicles 23:12–21)

How old was Joash when he became king? (2 Chronicles 24:1)

How long did Joash do what was right in God's eyes? (2 Kings 12:2)

Compare the kings of Israel and Judah listed in 2 Kings 15.

What did Zechariah prophesy against Joash? (2 Chronicles 24:20)

How did the king respond? (2 Chronicles 24:21)

Are parents to die for their children's sins, or children to die for their parents' sins? (2 Chronicles 25:4; Deuteronomy 24:16)

A NOTE FROM YOUR BIBLE STUDY MENTOR

By now you have a basic knowledge of the nations of Israel and Judah, both Hebrew people. What's next in lesson 12, the second part of 2 Kings/ 2 Chronicles?

Israel does not have long as a country. How will that nation end? Are there prophecies of restoration?

Among the kings of Israel's sister nation Judah, there stands out a godly king named Hezekiah. Will he have enough influence to keep his country from following the evil ways of Israel?

2 KINGS/2 CHRONICLES
God Blesses Loyalty

Israel rejected God, and Assyria invaded, destroying their country. God sent the prophets Micah, Nahum, Habakkuk, and Zephaniah, but the people ignored their warnings. Judah remained a nation for about 140 years before it fell to an invasion from Babylon.

2 Kings	2 Chronicles
Ch. 15 Azariah reigns in Judah, Zechariah reigns in Israel	Ch. 26–28; read Micah
	Ch. 26 (see Isaiah 1:1)
	Ch. 27
Ch. 16 Ahaz reigns in Judah	Ch. 28
Ch. 17 Hoshea reigns in Israel, Israel is conquered and people relocated to Assyria. Assyria sends people from other conquered countries to resettle Israel.	
Ch. 18 Hezekiah reigns in Judah	Ch. 29–31
Ch. 19 Hezekiah's plea to God for deliverance from Sennacherib	Ch. 32
Ch. 20 Hezekiah's remaining life	
Ch. 21 Manasseh reigns in Judah	Ch. 33 read Nahum
Ch. 22 Godly Josiah	Ch. 34–35 read Zephaniah
Ch. 23 Josiah restores true worship (see Jeremiah 1:2; read Habakkuk)	
Ch. 24 Judah overrun by Babylon (see Daniel Ch. 1)	
Ch. 25 Fall of Judah (see Ezekiel 1:1–3)	Ch. 36

PEOPLE, PLACES, HAPPENINGS

How long did Uzziah prosper? (2 Chronicles 26:5)

What was the result of Uzziah's pride? (2 Chronicles 26:16–21)

What happened the year Uzziah died? (Isaiah 6:1)

What did Ahaz make his son do? (2 Kings 16:3)

What happened to Hoshea when he refused to pay tribute to the King of Assyria? (2 Kings 17:4)

What happened to the country of Israel? (2 Kings 17:6)

Why? (2 Kings 17:7–12)

Had God warned them? How? (2 Kings 17:13–14)

What people resettled Israel? (2 Kings 17:24)

How did the tribes of Asher, Ephraim, Manasseh, and Zebulun respond to the king's runners? (2 Chronicles 30:10–11)

Describe Hezekiah's reign. (2 Chronicles 31:20–21)

What did Hezekiah do when threatened by Sennacherib? (2 Kings 19:14–19)

What was the reason Hezekiah prayed? (2 Kings 19:19)

How did God deliver Judah? (2 Kings 19:35; 2 Chronicles 32:21)

What was Isaiah's prophecy to Hezekiah? (2 Kings 20:1–2)

What was Hezekiah's response? (2 Kings 20:3)

How did God answer Hezekiah's prayer? (2 Kings 20:4–11)

Why calamity on Judah? (2 Kings 22:17)

What kind of king was Josiah? (23:25; 2 Chronicles 34:27)

How long did the people serve God? (2 Chronicles 34:33)

What prophet mourned for Josiah? (2 Chronicles 35:25)

How long did Jehoahaz reign? (2 Kings 23:31–34)

What happened to him? (2 Chronicles 36:1–4)

Did King Zedekiah respect Jeremiah's word from God? (2 Chronicles 36:12)

Whom did he rebel against? (2 Kings 24:20; 2 Chronicles 36:13)

Did God send warnings to His people? _____ Why? (2 Chronicles 36:15)

What was the people's response to the messengers? (2 Chronicles 36:16)

What happened to Zedekiah? (2 Kings 25:1–7)

What happened to Jerusalem? (2 Kings 25:9–10; 2 Chronicles 36:19)

How long was Judah to be in captivity? (2 Chronicles 36:21)

A NOTE FROM YOUR BIBLE STUDY MENTOR

At this time, Israel has fallen to a conquering nation and her people taken away. Hezekiah did not have a strong enough influence to keep his nation, Judah, from following Israel. Now they have been invaded, and the best of her people have been carried away to Babylon and other countries ruled by Babylon.

In the next lesson, you will learn about one young man, Daniel, who was taken captive and what his life was like.

DANIEL
Captive to Babylon

Daniel, a young Hebrew man, was captured when the Babylonian king, Nebuchadnezzar, invaded Judah. Daniel had visions for that time, as well as, for the future. The book of Daniel is part history and part prophecy. This study does not attempt to interpret his visions or their meanings. That is for another in–depth study.

Ch. 1 Daniel's new life and his three friends.

Ch. 2 Nebuchadnezzar's dream and interpretation

Ch. 3 Gold statue

Ch. 4 Nebuchadnezzar's second dream and interpretation

Ch. 5 Belshazzar's unusual experience

Ch. 6 Conspiracy against Daniel

Ch. 7–8 Two visions

Ch. 9 Daniel intercedes for his people (compare with Solomon's prayer in 1 Kings 8:22–52)

Ch. 10 Vision of an amazing man

Ch. 11–12 More prophecies

PEOPLE, PLACES, HAPPENINGS

What did Daniel purpose in his heart not to do? (1:8)

How did God reward Daniel and his friends? (1:17)

Was the king impressed? (1:18–20)

What did Daniel decide to do when the king purposed to kill all the wise men? (2:17–18)

What secret did Daniel reveal to the king? (2:27–28)

How was Daniel rewarded? (2:48)

In standard measurements, how big was Nebuchadnezzar's statue? (3:1)

Who refused to bow? (3:12, 19)

Were they harmed? (3:25)

What was Nebuchadnezzar's attitude? (4:30)

What happened to the king? (4:32)

How did this change him? (4:37)

What frightened Belshazzar? (5:5–6)

Who was able to interpret the writing? (5:11–12)

Why was he the only one who could interpret for the king? (5:11)

How was Belshazzar like his father? (5:21–23)

What was Daniel's reaction to the new decree? (6:10)

Did God deliver him? (6:22)

Describe the first beast Daniel saw in his vision. (7:4)

Describe the second beast Daniel saw. (7:5)

Describe the third beast Daniel saw. (7:6)

Describe the fourth beast Daniel saw. (7:7)

Describe the vision of the Ancient of Days. (7:9–10)

What do the four beasts represent? (7:17)

Where was Daniel in his second vision? (8:2; see Esther 1:2)

What time did his second visions refer to? (8:17–19)

What did the ram represent? (8:20)

What did the goat represent? (8:21)

Why does Daniel intercede? (9:18)

What two angels are mentioned by Daniel? (9:21, 10:21) Compare Luke 1:19, 26; Jude 9; Revelation 12:7

Compare Daniel 12:1 with Philippians 4:3 and Revelation 20:15; 21:27. What is mentioned in each of those references?

When Daniel wanted an explanation, what did the man clothed in linen say to him? (12:8–9)

How many days from the removal of daily sacrifice to the abomination of desolation? (12:11)

A NOTE FROM YOUR BIBLE STUDY MENTOR

Before Israel was destroyed, God sent prophets to warn them of impending disaster if they refused to repent. Sometimes He used a prophet's personal life as an object lesson as He did with Hosea. He was told to marry a prostitute.

Another prophet was reluctant to proclaim God's message; he tried to run away.

I hope you enjoy learning from these prophets as you broaden your knowledge of the Bible.

HOSEA, AMOS, OBADIAH, JONAH

God Speaks to His People

God spoke to His people through these "minor" prophets during the time recorded in 2 Kings 14, and 2 Chronicles 21 and 26. Before we get too far from the later days of Israel and Judah, it would be good to see what God spoke to His people through these prophets. Life as a prophet was not easy. God expected the prophet to proclaim His message, sometimes with his own life.

HOSEA
God wants His wandering bride to come back

Ch. 1 Hosea's wife and children

Ch. 2 God loves Israel even though they are unfaithful

Ch. 3 God wants Israel to return to Him

Ch. 4 Lawless Israel

Ch. 5 When life is difficult they will seek God

Ch. 6 Hosea calls for repentance

Ch. 7 Israel looks to other countries for help rather than to God

Ch. 8 Israel has rejected God

Ch. 9 God will not bless them while they rebel against Him

Ch. 10 Israel will reap what they sow

Ch. 11 God loves Israel, but His heart is breaking

Ch. 12 God reminisces about Jacob (Israel)

Ch. 13 After God brought them out of Israel they were disloyal

Ch. 14 God pleads for them to return so He can bless them

PEOPLE, PLACES, HAPPENINGS

Why did God tell Hosea to take a harlot for his wife? (1:2)

What did the birth of Jezreel foretell? (1:4)

What did Lo–Ruhamah mean? (1:6)

What did Lo–Ammi mean? (1:9)

Who did she forget? (2:13)

What charge did God bring against Israel? (4:1)

Why won't the people find the Lord? (5:6)

When would God respond to them? (5:15)

What did Hosea say to the people? (6:1–3)

Why was God displeased with Israel? (8:4)

What did God tell them to do? (10:12)

What did they do wrong? (10:13)

Though they were bent on backsliding, could God give them up? (11:7–8)

Had God left them alone all these years? (12:9–10)

What happened as a result of their prosperity? (13:4–6)

What did Hosea encourage the people to do to prevent further calamity? (14:1–3)

What will God do? (14:4)

AMOS
Seek the Lord

Ch. 1 Judgments against nations who mistreated Israel

Ch. 2 Judgments against Moab, Judah, and Israel

Ch. 3 God uses His prophet to proclaim His message

Ch. 4 Israel refuses to return to God

Ch. 5 Amos calls the people to seek God and live

Ch. 6 Warning against trusting in their apparent prosperity

Ch. 7 Amos defends his calling to be a prophet

Ch. 8 Israel hurries through what God has asked so they can do what they want

Ch. 9 After destruction, a time of blessing will come when God restores Israel

PEOPLE, PLACES, HAPPENINGS

How many groups of people did God prophesy against through Amos in chapters 1–2? List them.

Who did the Lord, through Amos, speak against in chapter 3? Why?

What five punishments did God cause in hopes His people will turn back to Him? (4:6, 7, 9, 10, 11)

Who were the people dealing with in this passage? (4:13)

What did Amos ask the people to do that they might live? (5:4, 6, 14)

Who was king at this time? (7:10; 2 Kings 14:23)

Was Amos a self–appointed prophet? (7:14–15)

Could anyone hide from coming destruction? (9:2–4) Compare with Psalm 139:7–12.

OBADIAH
What you have done will come back to you

PEOPLE, PLACES, HAPPENINGS

Who are the people of Edom? (Genesis 36)

Why did God speak through Obadiah the calamity to Edom? (v. 11–14)

JONAH
God wants all to repent

Ch. 1 Jonah runs from God

Ch. 2 God hears Jonah's prayer

Ch. 3 People of Nineveh respond to Jonah's preaching

Ch. 4 Jonah is angry at God

PEOPLE, PLACES, HAPPENINGS

Why was Jonah in trouble? (1:2–3)

Did he finally obey? (3:3)

How did the people respond to his preaching? (3:5–10)

Was Jonah happy with the results? (4:1)

How did God respond to Jonah's anger? (4:10–11)

A NOTE FROM YOUR BIBLE STUDY MENTOR

The next lesson includes four minor prophets, minor because their books are short, not that their message is less important. A lot can be learned about the character of God from what He spoke through these men.

I especially like Habakkuk. Boldly he questioned God, then respectfully waited to see how God would answer him. He must have had great trust in God.

Your Bible knowledge is growing. Keep up the good work!

MICAH, NAHUM, HABAKKUK, ZEPHANIAH
God's Message

To understand the life and times of these prophets read the following passages:

Micah	2 Chronicles 21–32; 2 Kings 15
Nahum	2 Chronicles 24; 2 Kings 21
Habakkuk	2 Chronicles 34–35; 2 Kings 22–23
Zephaniah	2 Chronicles 34–35; 2 Kings 22–23

The people of God drifted away from Him. No longer acknowledging their need of Him, they worshiped idols and welcomed false prophets. God warned them of coming disaster if they didn't return to Him, the God who was "merciful and gracious, long-suffering, and abounding in goodness and truth." (Exodus 34:6)

MICAH
Mourning and warning for Israel's sins. Israel's restoration

Ch. 1 Micah mourns the coming disaster of Israel and Judah

Ch. 2 Other prophets speak falsely

Ch. 3 Leaders and prophets are evil

Ch. 4 Future Israel

Ch. 5 Messiah is prophesied

Ch. 6 God questions their evil ways

Ch. 7 Micah confesses the sins of Israel

PEOPLE, PLACES, HAPPENINGS

Who was Micah's contemporary? (Jeremiah 26:18)

How did Micah describe the Lord's displeasure? (1:2–4)

Why was God angry at the prophets? (3:5)

Micah spoke of a future time. How did he see the future? (4:3)

How was the future Messiah mentioned? (5:2; see Luke 2:4–7; Matthew 2:1–6)

Did God want sacrifices from the people? (6:6–7)

What did God require of His people? (6:8)

When Micah saw the evil in his people, what did he do? (7:7)

What is God like in the end? (7:18–19)

NAHUM
Prophecy against God's enemy, Nineveh

Ch. 1 Who is as powerful as God?
Ch. 2 A display of God's power
Ch. 3 God is against Nineveh

PEOPLE, PLACES, HAPPENINGS

This prophecy is against what place? (1:1)

God is jealous and avenges, but . . .? (1:3)

God can be fiercely angry, but . . .? (1:7)

Why woe to Nineveh? (3:1–4)

HABAKKUK
The prophet questioned God and politely waited for God's response

Ch. 1 God is sovereign

Ch. 2 Trouble for those who cause trouble

Ch. 3 In spite of coming doom, Habakkuk trusts God

PEOPLE, PLACES, HAPPENINGS

What were the questions Habakkuk had for God? (1:1–4)

How did God answer? (1:5–11)

What were Habakkuk's next questions? (1:12–17)

Describe Habakkuk's attitude. (2:1)

God answers in 2:2–20 woes to five different people. What have they done wrong?

Compare 2:3–4 with Hebrews 10:37–38. How are they alike?

Although much devastation is coming, what did Habakkuk say? (3:17–19)

ZEPHANIAH
Prophecy of impending judgment and God's future world

Ch. 1 The day of the Lord's wrath

Ch. 2 Those who trust in false gods will be punished

Ch. 3 Those who are loyal to God are encouraged to wait on Him

PEOPLE, PLACES, HAPPENINGS

How was he related to Hezekiah? (1:1)

Who was God angry with? (1:6, 12, 17)

Zephaniah called the people to do what? (2:1–3)

Woe to those who had not done what? (3:2)

God will restore how? (3:8, 9, 12, 13)

A NOTE FROM YOUR BIBLE STUDY MENTOR

Wow! You have completed one-fourth of this study. Take a minute to consider all you now know. Amazing, right?!

The next few lessons will be about two major prophets—major because of the size of their books.

Isaiah is the first prophet you will study. What an awesome book! There is much treasure in this book.

In lesson sixteen, you will read prophecies concerning a coming Messiah, experience what Isaiah felt when he had a spectacular vision, and even get a quick glimpse of how Satan started out as an angel.

ISAIAH

Part 1: All Will Bow Before the Lord God

We will pause to consider what Isaiah and Jeremiah prophesied before continuing our Old Testament study.

Isaiah prophesied during the reigns of Uzziah, Jotham, Ahaz, and Hezekiah, kings of Judah (Isaiah 1:1). Compare with 2 Chronicles chapters 26–32 and 2 Kings chapters 15—20. Uzziah, Jotham's father (2 Kings 15:7; 2 Chronicles 26:23) also went by the name of Azariah. The Gospel of John quoted Isaiah in John 12: 38–41. Isaiah is considered a major prophet because of the size of the book.

Ch. 1 God's complaint against Judah was they had rebelled against Him, their times of worship were empty, just ritual

Ch. 2 Worship is due God

Ch. 3 God's judgment on Judah and Jerusalem

Ch. 4 A time of prosperity

Ch. 5 His disappointing vine, Judah

Ch. 6 Isaiah sees the Lord and overhears a heavenly conversation (see Genesis 1:26)

Ch. 7 War against Judah; (compare with 2 Kings 16:5 and 2 Chronicles 28:6)

Ch. 8 Assyria will invade; God's word to Isaiah

Ch. 9 Messianic prophecy (9:6–7), more destruction coming; His kingdom (compare Luke 2:11, Matthew 3:2; 6:33; 28:18; John 3:3, 5; 18:36–37)

Ch. 10 More woes on people who do wrong

Ch. 11 The future of Israel and the world; (compare 11:2 with John 1:32)

Ch. 12 A hymn of praise

Ch. 13 Compare 13:17 with Daniel 5:28–31

Ch. 14 Fall of Babylon and a picture of the fall of Lucifer; (compare with Luke 10:18)

PEOPLE, PLACES, HAPPENINGS

What specifically did God have against His people? (1:2, 4, 11, 12)

What did God ask of the people? (1:16–18)

If they were obedient, what did He promise? (1:19–20)

Could the idols save them? (2:20–21)

What did He say about their leaders? (3:12)

Was God happy with Judah? (5:7)

A NOTE FROM YOUR BIBLE STUDY MENTOR

Has your knowledge of the character of God expanded?

What's next? After prophecies against several nearby nations, the prophecies turn positive concerning the future. God promises to restore Judah in part two of Isaiah.

Oh, and there will be another miracle in nature. Can time stand still? Can it go backward? Although you learned about Hezekiah in lesson twelve, more of his story is recorded by Isaiah.

ISAIAH

Part 2: Powerful God Loves His People

Isaiah spoke of a coming righteous ruler who would bring peace. He prophesied against surrounding nations and told of the future restoration of Israel.

Ch. 15–23 Prophecies against various nations

Ch. 24 Future of the earth

Ch. 25 Promises for the future; (Compare 25:8 with Revelation 7:17)

Ch. 26–27 Song about the goodness of God

Ch. 28–29 Prophecies against Ephraim and Jerusalem

Ch. 30 God's people do not want Him

Ch. 31 Not trusting God

Ch. 32 A time of peace is coming

Ch. 33 The Lord is King and will save them

Ch. 34 Destruction coming to nations

Ch. 35 A time of prosperity

Ch. 36–39 Hezekiah's life extended (see 2 Kings 18–20; 2 Chronicles 29–32)

Ch. 40–41 God is strong and will help

Ch. 42–43 Redeemer of Israel

Ch. 44 There is no other God (Compare 44:6; 41:4; 43:11–12; 45:5–6; Revelation 1:8, 17; 22:13)

Ch. 45 God has made everything and everyone

Ch. 46 Futility of idols

Ch. 47 Babylon is brought low

Ch. 48 God's dealings with Israel

PEOPLE, PLACES, HAPPENINGS

What country did Isaiah prophesy against in chapters 15–16?

Why the proclamation against Israel? (17:10)

How are the people of Ethiopia described? (18:7)

What will happen to Egypt? (19:22)

What calamity will follow them? (20:6)

What did God ask of His people? (22:12)

How would they respond? (22:13)

How will judgment fall equally? (24:1–2)

What will happen to the earth? (24:19–20)

Who will God keep in perfect peace? (26:3)

What have they done wrong in 29:13–16?

How will it end for them in the future? (29:22–24)

What did the people tell the prophets sent by God? (30:10–11)

What did God tell the people? (30:15, 18)

What will the future land be like? (35:1–2)

What did Hezekiah do when he received a letter telling of a coming invasion? (37:14)

What did he pray? (37:15–20)

How big is God? (40:12, 15, 22)

Does God care about our problems? (40:27–30)

Who will be strong and not get weary? (40:31)

Who is the Servant in 42:1–4? (Compare with Luke 3:22; Matthew 17:5)

Who stretched out the heavens? (42:5)

Who else will be saved? (42:1, 6; Luke 2:32; John 10:16; Amos 9:12)

Is there another God? Is there another savior? (43:10–13; Hosea 13:4)

Will God forget our transgressions? (43:25–26)

What does 44:6 say? (see John 8:58 and Exodus 3:14)

Had God forgotten Israel? (44:21–22)

Can the created complain to the creator? (45:9–10)

Who created the earth and the heavens? (45:11–12, 18)

How can a person be saved? (45:22)

What did God say about idols? (46:5–7)

Why did God say He would put off His anger? (48:9)

Why did God discipline Israel? (48:10–11)

A NOTE FROM YOUR BIBLE STUDY MENTOR

You have learned a lot about God in this lesson. Your understanding of Him is growing. In the next lesson, Isaiah Pt. 3, you will learn even more about His character.

There are many prophecies concerning the future of God's people and many prophecies about the Messiah in the next lesson. Will those prophecies be fulfilled in the New Testament?

ISAIAH
Part 3: Returning Leads to Restoration

Through Isaiah, God promised to restore His people, if only they would repent and turn back to Him. He would send a Messiah that would take upon Himself all their sins, and would be a Messiah for the whole world. In the final chapters of Isaiah, God promised a prosperous Jerusalem in the future.

Ch. 49 His Servant will bring blessing

Ch. 50 His Servant will be mistreated

Ch. 51 Listen, my people (Compare 51:1 with Psalm 40:2)

Ch. 52 God will redeem His people

Ch. 53 The rejected Messiah

Ch. 54 Get ready to prosper

Ch. 55 God has what His people need

Ch. 56 Belonging to God is not limited to the Hebrews

Ch. 57 Sacrificing to other gods

Ch. 58 Doing right

Ch. 59 Prayers not answered because of sin

Ch. 60 Israel will be blessed

Ch. 61 Prosperous times

Ch. 62 Jerusalem restored

Ch. 63 Remembering their deliverance from Egypt

Ch. 64 They acknowledge their need for God

Ch. 65 Great times are coming

Ch. 66 God wants to help and bless

PEOPLE, PLACES, HAPPENINGS

How did God promise not to forget Israel? (49:14–16)

Who was their Savior? (49:26)

Who was mentioned in 50:6? (see Matthew 26:67; 27:30)

Should they be afraid of what people say? (51:7)

Who was mentioned? (52:13–14; 50:6; Matthew 26:67)

Why was He stricken? (53:8)

What did He carry? (53:12)

Will God be angry forever? (54:8)

What is the living water? (55:1; John 7:37–38)

What is important? (55:2–3)

What were they urged to do? (55:6–7)

Are human thoughts like God's thoughts? Explain. (55:8–9)

Who inhabits eternity? (57:15)

Who will He live with? (57:15)

What did God want instead of their self–directed fasts? (58:6–7)

Why would God not hear? (59:1–2; see Proverbs 28:9)

What displeased God? (59:15–16)

Compare 61:1–3 with Luke 4:16–19. Who is it talking about?

What does God do for those who wait for Him? (64:4)

Does anyone call on God? (64:7)

Who is the potter? Who is the clay? (64:8)

Why will there be bad times for the people? (65:12)

When will God answer? (65:24)

Which animals will eat together? (65:25)

Where is God's throne? (66:1; Jeremiah 23:24; 1 Kings 8:27, 43)

Who does God look to help? (66:2; 57:15; Psalms 34:18; 51:17)

Since they had chosen their own ways, what would God do? Why? (66:4)

A NOTE FROM YOUR BIBLE STUDY MENTOR

This lesson concludes the study of Isaiah. Now you will learn about the next major prophet, Jeremiah. Does age have anything to do with being chosen by God to be a prophet? It would seem that being chosen by God to be a prophet would be a privilege. Does Jeremiah agree? What is life like for him?

JEREMIAH
Part 1: The Weeping Prophet

Jeremiah was called as a young man to be God's prophet during King Josiah's reign. He is known as the weeping prophet because he was so emotionally moved by the spiritual state of his country.

Ch. 1 Jeremiah is called to be a prophet (see 2 Chronicles 34–36)

Ch. 2 God questions His people

Ch. 3 God wants His people to come back to Him

Ch. 4 Massive invasion

Ch. 5 God's punishment doesn't get His people's attention

Ch. 6 Warning of coming invasion

Ch. 7 God has repeatedly sent messengers to His people throughout their history

Ch. 8 They have rejected God's word

Ch. 9 Jeremiah weeps for his people

Ch. 10 Idols are not living beings; simply pieces of wood

Ch. 11 God reminds them of the covenant He made with their ancestors (see Deuteronomy 27)

Ch. 12 Jeremiah talks with God

Ch. 13 Pride of Judah

Ch. 14 Jeremiah's concern for his people

Ch. 15 Jeremiah is sad (see 2 Chronicles 33)

PEOPLE, PLACES, HAPPENINGS

Who was Jeremiah's father? (1:1)

How early did God know Jeremiah? (1:5)

What was Jeremiah's response to God's calling? (1:6)

How did God encourage Jeremiah? (1:7–8)

What questions did God ask? (2:5, 8, 11, 17)

What terrible wrong had the people done? (2:13, 17, 31, 32)

Can iniquity (sin) be washed away with soap? (2:22)

What did God ask of them? (3:1, 7, 12, 14, 22)

What brought destruction upon the country? (4:18)

Compare 5:3 with Revelation 16:9, 11.

What astonishing thing happened in Judah? (5:30–31)

What did the people do when God sent warnings? (6:16–17, 19)

Did the people listen to the messengers God sent? Explain. (7:13, 23–26)

What can the wise boast(glory) in? (9:23–24)

Is there anyone like God? (10:6)

What did the people do about the covenant? (11:8)

What conspiracy was there among the people of Judah? (11:9–10)

What did Jeremiah ask God? (12:1)

Why was the land made desolate? (12:11)

What was the message of the hidden sash? (13:1–11)

What question did God ask at the end of 13:27?

What was Jeremiah concerned about? (14:13)

How did God respond? (14:14)

What was Jeremiah's complaint? (15:10, 18)

How did God respond to Jeremiah's complaints? (15:19–21)

A NOTE FROM YOUR BIBLE STUDY MENTOR

In today's church world, the title or position of a prophet can seem a privileged position. You've studied about several prophets by now. What do you think?

Have you ever regretted the day you were born? Jeremiah did. In the next lesson, Jeremiah Pt. 2, you will learn why he felt that way

JEREMIAH

Part 2: God's People Refuse to Listen to Jeremiah

Through Jeremiah, God continued to warn His people, but they refused to listen. The priests and false prophets wanted Jeremiah dead because he spoke the truth, which annoyed them.

Ch. 16 No marriage or children for Jeremiah

Ch. 17 Trust in God leads to success (see Psalm 1)

Ch. 18 God, the potter; people turn on Jeremiah

Ch. 19 Object lesson of a broken flask

Ch. 20 Jeremiah regrets the day he was born

Ch. 21–39 Prophecies concerning captivity (see 2 Chronicles 36)

Ch. 21 Their warfare will be turned against them

Ch. 22 Messages to the sons of Josiah

Ch. 23 False prophets

Ch. 24 The good and bad punished alike, but God will bring back the good

Ch. 25 Israel refuses to listen

Ch. 26 Jeremiah speaks to all in a public place; priests and false prophets want him killed

Ch. 27 The politically correct prophets are wrong

Ch. 28 Hananiah, false prophet

Ch. 29 Jeremiah's prophecy by mail

Ch. 30 Israel will be restored

Ch. 31 Life will be good once again; a new covenant (see Hebrews 8:8–12)

Ch. 32 Jeremiah imprisoned; after the captivity, the people will return to God

Ch. 33 God's covenant

Ch. 34 Freed slaves re-enslaved

Ch. 35 Rechabites obey their leader; an example to Israel

Ch. 36 Jeremiah's words recorded and read to princes; king rejects it

Ch. 37 Jeremiah accused of defecting to the enemy

Ch. 38 Jeremiah rescued from a dungeon

Ch. 39 Jerusalem is conquered

PEOPLE, PLACES, HAPPENINGS

Why did God not want Jeremiah to marry and have children? (16:2–4)

What brought on such calamity to Israel? (16:11–12)

Describe the person who trusts in the Lord. (17:7–8)

Why is it not wise to follow our hearts? (17:9–10)

Who can truly heal and save us? (17:14)

What did the potter do with the marred vessel? (18:4)

How bad was it going to get for Israel? (19:9)

Could Jeremiah keep from speaking what God had shown him? (20:9)

How bad was Jeremiah feeling? (20:14–18)

Compare 23:18 and 23:21–22. What would happen?

How big is God? (23:23–24; Isaiah 66:1)

Can anyone hide from God? (23:24; Psalm 139:7–10)

How long would they serve Babylon? (25:11–12)

Why was Jeremiah's life threatened? (26:8–11)

Who came to his rescue? (26:24)

How would they know which prophet was speaking the truth? (28:9)

Why did Hananiah die? (28:15–17)

What did they need to do to find God? (29:13)

What promise did God give Jeremiah? (30:1–3)

How long had God loved His people? (31:3)

What was the new covenant? (31:33–34)

Is anything too hard for God? (32:17; Luke 1:37; Genesis 18:14)

How long is God's covenant? (33:20–21, 25–26)

What did the Rechabites do that Israel didn't do? (35:15–16)

How did the princes react to Baruch's reading of Jeremiah's words? (36:14–19)

How did the king react to Baruch's reading of Jeremiah's words? (36: 23–24)

How long was Jeremiah to be kept in prison? (37:21; 38:9)

Who rescued Jeremiah from the dungeon? (38:7–13)

Was Jeremiah able to safely tell the king the truth of coming events? (38:14–28)

Did Jeremiah's prophecy come true? (39:4–9)

Why was Ebed–Melech protected? (39:16–18)

A NOTE FROM YOUR BIBLE STUDY MENTOR

You have now completed one-third of the lessons. Great job! You have achieved a lot and have greatly expanded your knowledge of the Bible. The next lesson ends your study of Jeremiah. What happens to Jeremiah? To his secretary(scribe)? Will Jeremiah still hope in God?

JEREMIAH/LAMENTATIONS

Part 3: Jeremiah Continues to Prophesy

This lesson concludes the study of the prophet Jeremiah and takes a look at Lamentations, which is commonly attributed to Jeremiah. It is his sad songs about the invasion of his country by the forces of Babylon, and the capture of many of his people. Even in calamity, the people refused to listen.

Ch. 40 Governor appointed for Jerusalem

Ch. 41 Revolt

Ch. 42 Jeremiah's prophecy

Ch. 43 Remnant of people go to Egypt

Ch. 44 God's warning to those who went to Egypt

Ch. 45 Baruch will be protected

Ch. 46 Egypt will be invaded

Ch. 47–50 Prophecies against neighboring nations

Ch. 51 Prophecy against Babylon (see Daniel Ch. 5)

Ch. 52 Summary of Jerusalem's downfall

PEOPLE, PLACES, HAPPENINGS

Who recognized that Judah's God was punishing His people? (40:1–2)

Was Jeremiah taken to Babylon? (40:1–6)

Who was the puppet governor of Jerusalem? (40:5)

Who killed Gedaliah, the governor? (41:2–4)

Did the people want to know what God asked of them? (42:1–6)

What was Jeremiah's prophecy concerning their desire to go to Egypt? (42:11–19)

Were they being honest in their request? (42:20)

What was the people's response? (43:1–4)

Was Jeremiah forced to go to Egypt with them? (43:6)

What was the men's response to Jeremiah's warning from God? (44:16)

Will God allow the captives to return to Judah? (46:27–28)

Jeremiah prophesies against what nations? (49:1, 7, 23, 28, 34)

What has happened to Israel? (50:17)

Why will God destroy Babylon? (50:29)

Who was coming from the north? (50:41–42)

Who will invade Babylon? (51:11; Daniel Ch. 5)

What happened to King Zedekiah when Judah was invaded? (52:8–11)

How many did Nebuchadnezzar take captive in the seventh year? (52:28)

How many did Nebuchadnezzar take captive in the eighteenth year? (52:29)

How many did Nebuchadnezzar take captive in the twenty–third year? (52:30)

LAMENTATIONS
Jeremiah Mourns

Ch. 1 Jerusalem has gravely sinned

Ch. 2 God is angry

Ch. 3 Jeremiah's hope is in God

Ch. 4 Shame has come upon Jerusalem (Zion)

Ch. 5 Intercession for their country to be restored

PEOPLE, PLACES, HAPPENINGS

Who was he lamenting? Why? (1:1–3)

What had the Lord done? (2:7)

How did Jeremiah react? (2:11)

Describe Jeremiah's reputation. (3:14)

What is Jeremiah's hope in spite of all the calamity? (3:22–24)

Did God cause the calamity willingly? (3:33)

Who were His people looking to for help? (4:17)

What did Jeremiah confess? (5:15–16)

After he saw the arrogance of his people, warned them for 40–50 years, and witnessed their downfall, what was Jeremiah's natural reaction? (5:19–22)

A NOTE FROM YOUR BIBLE STUDY MENTOR

Ezekiel had some extraordinary visions and experiences. You may not understand all the meanings of these, but you can certainly learn some interesting information about the people and increase your knowledge of the Bible.

In this book, God used many object lessons to get His message to His people. Even Ezekiel's life was an object lesson.

EZEKIEL

Part 1: Dramatic Visions for Ezekiel

Ezekiel was a contemporary of Jeremiah, Daniel, and Obadiah. He was among the Jews captured and taken to Babylon. As the prophet of Jehovah God, he had some spectacular visions and experiences. Ezekiel prophesied to those in captivity with him and prophesied about events in the distant future that would happen in the last days.

Ch. 1 Vision of a whirlwind

Ch. 2 Ezekiel sent to prophesy

Ch. 3 Scroll becomes food

Ch. 4 Model of Jerusalem under siege

Ch. 5 The prophet shaves his head and beard

Ch. 6 Ezekiel talks to the mountains

Ch. 7 Israel's collapse

Ch. 8 The prophet is shown disturbing activities

Ch. 9 People who are loyal to God are marked and protected

Ch. 10 God's glory leaves the temple

Ch. 11 God promises to bring the people back to their homeland

Ch. 12 God uses Ezekiel as an object lesson (see 2 Kings 25:4)

PEOPLE, PLACES, HAPPENINGS

When did Ezekiel see his first vision? (1:1; 2 Chronicles 36:20–21)

Where was he when he saw his first vision? (1:3)

What color was the whirlwind? (1:4) _____

Each creature had four _____ and four _____. (1:6)

When they moved what did it sound like? (1:24; Revelation 1:15)

What was above the creatures? (1:26)

Who was Ezekiel sent to? (2:1–3)

How was he encouraged? (2:6)

What did the scroll taste like? (3:3)

After Ezekiel was transported to Tel Abib, how long did he sit stunned and astonished? (3:15)

Under what circumstances would God hold Ezekiel accountable? (3:18–19)

Ezekiel was to lie on his side for _____ days for Israel and _____ days for Judah. (4:5–6)
What were the ingredients in this bread? (4:9)

Why did God punish Jerusalem? (5:6)

How would the surrounding nations react to what is happening to Jerusalem? (5:15)

How did their adulteries and disloyalty affect God? (6:9)

If they stayed in the besieged city, what would happen to them? (7:15; 2 Kings 25)

If they left the city, what would happen to them? (7:15)

How did Ezekiel get to an area between heaven and earth? (8:3)

What were the 25 men in the inner court worshiping? (8:16; Deuteronomy 4:19; Jeremiah 2:27)

Who was to remain untouched, safe? (9:6)

Why were Israel and Judah so perverse? (9:9)

What was the man in linen to take from among the cherubim? (10:6)

What were the cherubim full of? (10:12)

What would God do with the remnant of people? (11:19–20)

Why didn't the people see or hear? (12:2)

When would they know that He is the Lord? (12:15)

A NOTE FROM YOUR BIBLE STUDY MENTOR

I don't think I would want to be a prophet in those days. Life didn't go well for them if the people didn't like the message they proclaimed.

In this next lesson, Ezekiel's wife dies, yet he is not allowed to mourn. What sadness he must have felt.

EZEKIEL

Part 2: Then You Shall Know That I Am the Lord God

When their lives lay in ruin and the Hebrews realized Ezekiel was right, they would return to the Lord God. They would find God waiting to welcome them back.

Ch. 13 You shall know that I am the Lord God

Ch. 14 Idolatry is wrong

Ch. 15 Desolate land

Ch. 16 God made His people and His city beautiful, but His people left Him like an adulterous wife

Ch. 17 Whatever happens, God is still in control

Ch. 18 Turn away from sin to God and live

Ch. 19 Israel is brought low

Ch. 20 God promises that one day they will see the error of their ways and He will bring them back

Ch. 21 Babylon will be used to bring destruction

Ch. 22 God looked for one to stand in the gap for Israel

Ch. 23 Ezekiel's prophecy compares Samaria and Jerusalem to two sisters

Ch. 24 Ezekiel's wife dies, but he is not allowed to mourn; he is an object lesson

Ch. 25 Warnings to surrounding nations

Ch. 26 Prophecy against Tyre

Ch. 27 Lament for Tyre

Ch. 28 Fall of Lucifer

Ch. 29 Egypt will be attacked

Ch. 30 Egypt's allies will fall with Egypt

Ch. 31 Egypt compared to a great tree

Ch. 32 Lament for Egypt

PEOPLE, PLACES, HAPPENINGS

What would be the result of God's actions against the false prophets? (13:9, 21, 23)

Will the righteousness of one person save another person? Explain. (14:14, 16, 18, 20)

Why would God make the land desolate? (15:8)

Had Jerusalem been admired by surrounding nations? (16:14)

What grievous sin did they commit? (16:20–21; 2 Chronicles 28:1–3)

Will a parent pay for the child's sin, or will the child pay for the parent's sin? (18:9, 13, 17, 19–20)

Is God pleased when the sinner dies in his sin? (18:30–32)

How far back in their history had Israel been rebelling against God? (20:8)

What phrase is repeated in chapter 20? (20:12, 20, 26, 38, 42, 44)

What would God do with His rebellious people? (22:15)

Who did God look for? (22:30)

Who do the sisters represent? (23:4)

Why were the sisters punished? (23:35)

Who did the prophet's wife represent? (24:15–21)

Who were the four nations Ezekiel speaks against? (25:2, 9, 12, 15)

What will happen to Tyre? (26:19; 27:32)

Why prophesy against the prince of Tyre? (28:2)

Compare 28:11–15 with Isaiah 14:12–17 and Luke 10:18. Who is being described?

What will Israel's future be like? (28:25–26)

Who were Egypt's allies? (30:5)

Who would come against Egypt? (30:10–12)

What would God do with the Egyptians? (30:26)

What phrase is repeated in chapters 28–30? (28:24, 26; 29:9, 16, 21; 30:25)

What will happen to Egypt? (31:1–13)

Why do you think many nations would be afraid when Babylon conquered Egypt? (32:9–10)

A NOTE FROM YOUR BIBLE STUDY MENTOR

In part three, Ezekiel prophesied about the future temple in Jerusalem—how it was to be built, who could enter it, and what kind of worship was to be performed.

EZEKIEL
Part 3: Israel Will Be Restored

Ezekiel prophesied that the people willingly followed their leaders who led them astray. In His time, God would restore Israel and repair the damage they had done to His name.

Ch. 33 Ezekiel is chosen to be a watchman

Ch. 34 Irresponsible leaders (see John 10:1–34; Isaiah 40:11)

Ch. 35 Word against people in Mt. Seir for their boasting against God

Ch. 36 God will restore their land and cleanse His people's sin

Ch. 37 Dry bones brought to life

Ch. 38 Prophecy against a northern king, Gog

Ch. 39 Gog and his terrible horde will be destroyed

Ch. 40–43 Precise plans for a new temple

Ch. 44 Rules for those who enter the temple

Ch. 45 Area surrounding the temple

Ch. 46 Laws for offerings and worship

Ch. 47 Healing water, borders of the land

Ch. 48 Land divided among the tribes

PEOPLE, PLACES, HAPPENINGS

Will God hold Ezekiel responsible for getting His message to the people? Explain. (33:1–9)

Who will be saved—the good who sin, or the wicked who repent and turn from sin? (33:12–19; Matthew 21:28–31; James 1:22)

What did God have against the shepherds of His people? (34:3–4)

What will God do to help? (34:23–24)

Why prophesy against Mt. Seir? (35:5)

Why was God against His people? (36:18–21)

When will the nations know that He is the Lord God? (36:23)

What will God do with Israel in the end? (36:24–30)

What was in the valley? (37:1)

What was Ezekiel to prophesy? (37:3–6)

What do the two sticks represent? (37:19)

How did that prophecy apply to Israel? (37:21–22)

Where will Gog come from and how big is his army? (38:15)

When will Gog attack Israel? (38:16)

How bad will the earthquake be? (38:19–20)

What will rain down on the troops of Gog? (38:22)

What will happen after the defeat of Gog? (39:7)

How long will it take to bury the dead from the war with Gog? (39:12)

During the 25th year of their captivity, where was Ezekiel taken in a vision? (40:1–2)

What was on each gatepost in the temple? (40:16)

Describe the glory of God he saw. (43:1–3)

What happened to the eastern gate? Why? (44:1–2)

Which priests will God allow to minister before Him? (44:15)

When would the gate facing east be opened? (46:1)

How many gates are there in the city? (48:30–34)

Will the gates have names for ease of identification? (48:31)

Name the gates for the north side. (48:31)

Name the gates for the east side. (48:32)

Name the gates for the south side. (48:33)

Name the gates for the west side. (48:34)

What will be the name of that future city? (48:35)

A NOTE FROM YOUR BIBLE STUDY MENTOR

The next lesson is about Esther, a young girl chosen to be queen. Was she excited about being chosen? Why did the king need a new queen? What happened to the other queen? Will life be a bed of roses for Esther? Will her life be in danger?

ESTHER
For Such a Time As This

King Ahasuerus (Ezra 4:6) was in control when a dispute arose in Jerusalem about the rebuilding of the temple. Esther was an orphan brought up by an older cousin during this time. As we shall see, she played an important role in Jewish history.

Ch. 1 Queen Vashti refuses the king's request

Ch. 2 Search for a new queen leads to an orphaned Jewish girl

Ch. 3 Haman's pride causes confusion in the city of Shushan

Ch. 4 Esther rises to the occasion

Ch. 5 Esther's plan

Ch. 6 The king remembers Mordecai

Ch. 7 Haman's punishment

Ch. 8 Decree sent to protect Jews

Ch. 9 Jewish holiday of Purim established

Ch. 10 Mordecai's promotion

PEOPLE, PLACES, HAPPENINGS

Who was the king? (1:1–2)

Who was the queen? (1:9)

What did he do when he got drunk? (1:10–11)

How did the queen respond? (1:12)

How did the king react to her refusal? (1:13–19)

Since he couldn't see the queen, what was suggested? (2:2–4)

What relation was Esther to Mordecai? (2:7)

Who was chosen to be queen? (2:17)

How did Mordecai act toward Haman? (3:2)

How did Haman seek revenge? (3:8, 13)

What did Esther do when she heard of the plan? (4:8–11)

How did Mordecai advise her? (4:13–14)

Describe Esther's preparation for her role? (4:16–17)

What was Haman's thoughts about the banquet? (5:11–12)

Haman's wife, Zeresh, suggested a plan. Describe it. (5:14)

Why was Mordecai honored? How? (6:1–11)

What did Esther request during the second banquet? (7:3–4)

What sealed Haman's fate? (7:8)

How did King Ahasuerus get around the decree he had previously made? (8:11)

What is the name of the holiday celebrated to memorialize this occasion? (9:26–28)

A NOTE FROM YOUR BIBLE STUDY MENTOR

After seventy years of captivity in a foreign country, the Jews were allowed to return to their native land of Israel.

Seventy years—a lifetime. In Lesson 26, we will learn who returns to their homeland. How old were they when they were taken? How old are they now? It sounds like a completely different group of people to me. Is it a fresh start for them?

In what condition will they find their capital city? Will the temple be rebuilt? What will happen to their culture?

EZRA, HAGGAI, ZECHARIAH
The People Return

In the book of Ezra, King Cyrus wanted the temple in Jerusalem rebuilt, so he sent many Jews back to Judah to complete that project. Haggai and Zechariah prophesied during this time. The seventy years of bondage was complete. Israel was restored.

EZRA
Help with the temple, people are counted

Ch. 1 Cyrus sends Jews back to Jerusalem to rebuild the temple

Ch. 2 Jews return

Ch. 3 Jeshua restores worship

Ch. 4 Adversaries cause trouble for the builders

Ch. 5 Rebuilding temple

Ch. 6 Original decree found

Ch. 7 Ezra comes with a letter full of support from King Artaxerxes

Ch. 8 Safe trip for those bringing much wealth from the king

Ch. 9 Ezra's prayer

Ch. 10 Shechaniah's solution

PEOPLE, PLACES, HAPPENINGS

Why did Cyrus send Jews back? (1:2)

What did he send back with them? (1:7–11)

How many returned? (2:64)

When did they begin work on the temple? (3:8)

Were the troublemakers successful? (4:6, 21)

By whose authority were they rebuilding the temple? (5:11, 13–14; Acts 4:18–20; 5:29)

What was Darius's response? (6:7–12)

What was Ezra's attitude? (7:10)

Why did Ezra pray for protection when he could have requested military protection from Artaxerxes? (8:22)

Why did Ezra tear his clothes? (9:1–3)

What was the tone of Ezra's prayer? (9:5–6)

Did he think God was fair in His dealings with His people? (9:13)

What was the people's attitude? (10:1)

HAGGAI
Encouragement for the builders of the temple

Ch. 1 A call to build God's house
Ch. 2 Haggai prophesied of a future temple, future blessing

PEOPLE, PLACES, HAPPENINGS

If they ignored God, what would their life be like? (1:6)

What was the response to Haggai's prophecy? (1:12)

How can the people be strong? (2:4)

ZECHARIAH
Coming deliverance for Judah

Ch. 1 God promises to be with His people if they will return to Him

Ch. 2 The Lord will come to establish His kingdom on earth

Ch. 3 Future Messiah

Ch. 4 Two olive trees, two anointed ones

Ch. 5 A flying scroll

Ch. 6 Four chariots

Ch. 7 Fasting and weeping for themselves or for God

Ch. 8 Jerusalem will be great again

Ch. 9 The coming king

Ch. 10 Judah will flourish

Ch. 11 Worthless shepherd

Ch. 12 God will defend Judah

Ch. 13 Refining of God's people

Ch. 14 The Day of the Lord

PEOPLE, PLACES, HAPPENINGS

When did Zechariah begin to prophesy? (1:1)

God warned His people to not be like their ancestors. Explain (1:3–4)

What color were the horses in his vision? (1:8)

Where was the man going with the measuring line? Why? (2:1–2)

What was the angel instructed to do for Joshua, the high priest? (3:3–5)

Who did the two olives trees represent? (4:11–14; Revelation 11:3–6)

What had God's people done that preceded their captivity? (7:11–12)

What will Jerusalem be called in the future? (8:3)

Why will ten men grasp the sleeve of a Jewish man? (8:23)

Who is mentioned in 9:9? (Compare with Matthew 21:1–11)

Why will God bring Judah back? (10:6)

What did the wages foretell? (11:12; Matthew 26:14–15)

In that day, what will God do to the nations that come against Jerusalem? (12:9)

How many will die? (13:8)

What will God do with the remaining one–third? (13:9)

When the Lord's feet touch the Mount of Olives, what will happen? (14:4)

A NOTE FROM YOUR BIBLE STUDY MENTOR

Another person stands out during this period of captivity: Nehemiah, a servant of the king. Nehemiah was so burdened about the condition of the capital of his homeland, Jerusalem, that he risked his life to share his concerns with the king.

Surprise! Surprise! The king gave his approval for rebuilding the city walls. Even with the support of the king, would the project go forward without a problem?

NEHEMIAH
Nehemiah Returns to Jerusalem

Nehemiah served King Artaxerxes as his cupbearer. He was also a devout leader in the Jewish community. When Nehemiah heard of the sad condition of his home city, he was greatly disturbed. The king gave him permission to return to Jerusalem and sent him back with a military escort. While rebuilding the walls and temple, they endured much opposition.

Ch. 1 Nehemiah's prayer (see 1 Kings 8:46–53; Deuteronomy 30:2–5)

Ch. 2 Nehemiah returns to Jerusalem

Ch. 3 Many people helped rebuild the walls of Jerusalem

Ch. 4 Builders are threatened by Sanballat, Tobiah, and the Arabs

Ch. 5 Poor oppressed (Compare with Deuteronomy 15:1–15)

Ch. 6 Rebuilding of the wall is completed

Ch. 7 Genealogy of those who returned (Compare 7:66 with Ezra 2:64)

Ch. 8 Ezra reads the Law (see Leviticus 23:33–36)

Ch. 9 Jews confess their sins and the sins of their fathers

Ch. 10 A covenant is written and signed by many people

Ch. 11 People assigned to live in the city, or in the surrounding area

Ch. 12 Dedication of the wall of Jerusalem

PEOPLE, PLACES, HAPPENINGS

Why was Nehemiah sad? (1:1–4)

Why was Nehemiah fearful? (2:1–3)

How long was he in Jerusalem before he revealed his purpose? (2:11–17)

Who was the Horonite? Ammonite? Arab? (2:19–20)

How did the Jews protect themselves and their work? (4:16–17)

Did Nehemiah expect to be fed at the governor's expense? (5:14–19)

What was Nehemiah's response to Sanballat's request for a meeting? (6:3)

How long did it take to complete the walls? (6:15)

Why were the surrounding nations afraid? (6:16)

How long did Ezra read the law? (8:3)

When was the last time the people kept the Feast of Tabernacles? (8:17)

When the people rebelled in the past, what did God do? Why? (9:17–19)

After the people were settled and prosperous in the new land, did they remain loyal to God? (9:26)

How did God respond to their impudent ways? (9:29–31)

Did the people think God treated them fairly? (9:33)

What percent agreed to live in Jerusalem? (11:1–2)

How many from the tribe of Judah would live in Jerusalem? (11:6)

How many from the tribe of Benjamin would live in Jerusalem? (11:8)

How many Levites? (11:18)

How many choirs were there? (12:31)

Could anyone go into the temple? (13:1)

What evil had Eliashib done while Nehemiah was absent? (13:4–7)

What did Nehemiah do? (13:8–9)

What did Nehemiah see on the Sabbath? (13:15)

What had they promised? (10:30–31)

Did they keep their word? (13:23–24)

A NOTE FROM YOUR BIBLE STUDY MENTOR

Joel is a short, but powerful book. Why does he sound the alarm?

Malachi, too, is a short book with a direct message. Does God get tired of some people? Why? Take a quick look at Lesson 28.

JOEL/MALACHI
Two Messengers

These two prophets, Joel and Malachi, lived either during the later years of captivity or after they had returned to Jerusalem. There are no dates or texts to link them to specific years. However, they both had important messages from God to His people.

JOEL
God calls His people to repentance

Ch. 1 The olden days were not golden

Ch. 2 The Day of the Lord is coming, repent.

Ch. 3 God will restore His people

PEOPLE, PLACES, HAPPENINGS

Joel was talking about what kind of devastation? (1:4)

What did Joel tell the priests to do? (1:13, 14)

Sound the alarm because what is coming? (2:2)

How do the local people respond to the invasion? (2:6)

Pray, "Spare your people . . . for the nations will wonder" what? (2:17)

God will restore what? (2:25)

In the book of Acts, who is quoting Joel 2:28–29? (Acts 2:17–21)

Who will be saved? (2:32)

Where will all the nations gather? (3:12)

What will happen to God's people during this time? (3:16)

MALACHI
God will protect His people if they will return to Him

Ch. 1 God discusses their behavior

Ch. 2 The priests have led the people astray

Ch. 3 The people will be able to discern good from evil

Ch. 4 The Day of the Lord will be great

PEOPLE, PLACES, HAPPENINGS

What did Malachi accuse the people of doing that displeased God? (1:7, 8, 13)

What kind of people were the Levites, the true priests? (2:5–7)

What does God hate? (2:16)

How have they wearied the Lord? (2:17)

What will God's messenger be like? (3:2–3)

Does God change? (3:6)

What will God do if they bring their tithes? (3:10–12)

Who receives the tithe? (Deuteronomy 14:22–29)

To those who fear the Lord, what will the "Day" be like for them? (4:2)

A NOTE FROM YOUR BIBLE STUDY MENTOR

The book of Job (pronounced with a long o sound) was originally written as a poem, so it is studied with other poetic books. It is believed he lived after Noah but before Abraham.

I'm sure you've heard the expression "the patience of Job." Is that an accurate description? As you study his life, maybe you will agree or disagree. When disaster strikes Job, will his wife support him? What about his friends?

JOB

Part 1: Job Learns to Trust God

Job's trust in God was sorely tried as he was allowed to go through some dark times. When all around him gave way, he learned to trust God. Since the time of Job is uncertain, for this study it is placed after the known history. What is fairly certain is that he probably lived between Noah and Abraham. Job is mentioned in James 5:11 in the New Testament. He is also mentioned in Ezekiel 14:14, 20. It is a poetic book in its original format so is placed with the other poetic books in the Bible.

Ch. 1 Job loses his children and livestock

Ch. 2 Job loses his health

Ch. 3 Job regrets the day he was born

Ch. 4–5 Eliphaz reminds Job how he has helped others

Ch. 6–7 Job pours out his anguish wanting to know what he has done wrong

Ch. 8 Bildad tells Job to repent

Ch. 9–10 Job acknowledges the sovereignty of God, yet he questions Him

Ch. 11 Zophar asks if Job can understand God

Ch. 12–14 Job states that God can do anything He chooses

Ch. 15 Eliphaz scolds Job for speaking his thoughts to God

Ch. 16–17 Job accuses his friends of being without sympathy

Ch. 18 Bildad hints to Job that he must have been wicked

Ch. 19 Job considers the idea that God may be against him

Ch. 20 Zophar preaches against evil

Ch. 21 Job tells his friends that evil people can prosper just like good people

---

PEOPLE, PLACES, HAPPENINGS

Did Job sin by accusing God of causing his loss? (1:22)

When his health was gone, what did Job's wife want him to do? (2:9)

How did Job feel about his life? (3:3, 11, 16)

Who did Elliphaz say was the happy person? (5:17)

What did Job ask? (7:20)

What did Bildad promise? (8:21)

Was there a mediator for Job during this Old Testament time? (9:33)

In the New Testament, who is the mediator? (1 Timothy 2:5)

Who made Job? (10:8–12)

How did Job answer Zophar? (12:3)

What is in God's hand? (12:10)

What does God have? (12:13)

God may do what? (13:15)

What will Job do anyway? (13:15)

In the light of all time, is man's life very long? (14:2)

According to Eliphaz, what condemns Job? (15:6)

What did Eliphaz ask Job? (15:7–9)

What did Job call his friends? (16:2)

Who was Bildad describing? (18:21)

What did Job know in spite of all his misfortune? (19:25–26)

Does death come to the good as well as the bad? (21:23–26)

A NOTE FROM YOUR BIBLE STUDY MENTOR

When everything in life falls apart, when all is lost, when bad things happen, and when no one understands, can Job still trust God? Can we still trust God?

JOB

Part 2: Job's Humility

Job's humility was evident in the later part of this book. After Elihu, the youngest scolded Job and his friends for their lack of faith, Job was confronted by God, speaking from a whirlwind.

Ch. 22 Eliphaz instructs Job to repent of his sinful ways

Ch. 23–24 Job responds (see 1 Peter 1:6–7)

Ch. 25 Bildad questions how a human can be righteous before God

Ch. 26–27 Job defends his integrity

Ch. 28 Where can wisdom be found?

Ch. 29 Compare chapter 29 with Eliphaz's accusations in chapter 22

Ch. 30 Those Job has helped in the past now see his fall

Ch. 31 Job analyzes his life searching for wrongdoing

Ch. 32 Elihu finally speaks after respectfully waiting for his elders to have their say

Ch. 33 God does what He wants

Ch. 34 Job is lacking in wisdom

Ch. 35 God is beyond the reach of our good or bad

Ch. 36 God is mighty and is aware of everyone

Ch. 37 Weather is a picture of God's majesty

Ch. 38 The Lord questions Job

Ch. 39 Does Job know anything about wild animals?

Ch. 40 Job is told to stand before God and pay attention

Ch. 41 Leviathan described

Ch. 42 Job humbles himself before God and repents of his words

PEOPLE, PLACES, HAPPENINGS

If Job could find God, what would he do? (23:3–5)

When God had tested Job, what would be the result? (23:10)

Is God blind to the ways of the evil? (24:23)

What did God hang the earth on? (26:7)

What did Job promise he would not do? (27:2–5)

Where can wisdom be found? (28:28)

What did Job wish for? (29:2–5)

What would be denying God and deserving of judgment? (31:24–28)

Why did Job's three friends stop talking with him? (32:1)

Why was Elihu angry? (32:2–3)

Why had Elihu waited to speak? (32:4–5)

Does God sin (commit iniquity)? (34:10, 12)

What would happen if God chose to keep His breath, His spirit, to Himself? (34:14–15)

Can those who commit wrong hide from God? (34:21–22)

Is the creator affected by our lives? (35:6–7)

Who is in charge of the weather? (37:2–12)

Out of what did God speak to Job? (38:1)

What constellations did God mention? (38:31–32)

What did God ask Job? (40:2)

How did Job respond? (40:3–5)

What beasts were mentioned? (40:15; 41:1)

How did Job respond to God's command in 40:7? (42:4–6)

Describe Job's life after this crisis. (42:10–17)

A NOTE FROM YOUR BIBLE STUDY MENTOR

A big congratulation to you! You are at the halfway point of this study of the Bible. Take a minute to think about all you've learned and how far you have come on this journey to gain a fundamental knowledge of the Bible. You have accomplished much.

Psalms are an excellent way to learn how to communicate with God. King David, who wrote many of the Psalms, speaks from his heart. He is a real human with real struggles. His enemies might have been real people, but we have enemies of our souls. Doubts, fears, anger, our sinful nature, conflicts with people, hopes crushed, etc. We can learn from David to go to God, to write our feelings or simply speak to God about what is bothering us. There are no secrets with God. He already knows. We are safe with Him.

PSALMS
Part 1: Book 1 • Psalms 1–41

Psalms Book 1 begins this series of lessons. Psalms were songs, prayers, and poems written over a period of about a thousand years. Some were written during the time of Moses. Most were written during the time of King David and King Solomon. Others were written during or after the exile. The Psalms are divided into five books. For this study, we will consider one book per lesson.

Ch. 1 Blessed is the person who is focused on God

Ch. 2 A Messianic psalm

Ch. 3–4 God keeps safe those who trust in Him

Ch. 5 A prayer for guidance

Ch. 6–7 David asks for faith in God's deliverance during difficult times

Ch. 8 David considers the beauty of God's creation

Ch. 9 Praise to God and a plea for protection from enemies

Ch. 10 God will win over evil

Ch. 11–14 Life may be difficult, but trust in God will triumph

Ch. 15 People who live rightly will dwell with God

Ch. 16–17 Our confidence is in God

Ch. 18 David expresses his gratitude for God's protection from Saul

Ch. 19 Creation speaks of God's ability

Ch. 20–21 Salvation

Ch. 22 A messianic psalm

Ch. 23 Shepherd of His people

Ch. 24 Who is like God?

Ch. 25–26 Prayer for deliverance and redemption

Ch. 27–29 God is David's light, his strength and is worthy of praise

Ch. 30–31 The Lord answers prayer and preserves His people

Ch. 32 Forgiveness

Ch. 33–34 It is good to trust in God

Ch. 35–36 God is the protector of His people

Ch. 37 Fret not

Ch. 38 David is weighed down by his sins

Ch. 39 David is trusting God for understanding and forgiveness

Ch. 40 God has brought David up from a very low time in his life

Ch. 41 David pleads for God to heal his soul

PEOPLE, PLACES, HAPPENINGS

Who is the happy/blessed person? (1:1)

What is the common phrase from 2:7 and Hebrews 1:5?

How did David indicate he is not worried? (3:5; 4:8)

Who did David trust completely? (11:1)

Describe the words of the Lord? (12:6)

What has the fool said? (14:1)

What is the Lord searching for when He looks down from heaven? (14:2)

Who counsels David? (16:7)

Why did David call on the Lord? (17:6)

Where can we see the Lord's handiwork? (19:1–3)

What is perfect, sure, right, and pure? (19:7–8)

What would be a good prayer for the words we say? (19:14)

Compare 22:1 with Mark 15:34 Who is it talking about?

What is the occasion? (Compare with Matthew 27, Mark 15, Luke 23, John 19)

What other verses foretell the crucifixion? (22:8, 14, 16–18)

Who is the good shepherd? (23:1)

What belongs to the Lord? (24:1)

What did David desperately want God to do for him? (25:7, 11, 18)

Why was David happy? (28:6–7)

What did David have that was in God's hands? (31:15)

Who is the blessed/happy person? (32:1)

Who is the Lord near to? (34:18; Isaiah 66:2)

How many times in Psalm 37 are we told not to fret?

God brought David out of what? (40:2)

A NOTE FROM YOUR BIBLE STUDY MENTOR

When King David commits sin, does he try to hide it or look for excuses? Explore Lesson 32, Psalms Pt. 2.

PSALMS
Part 2: Book 2 • Psalms 42–72

In Psalms Book 2, the first nine psalms of this book were written by worship leaders for Asaph and Korah. The next fifteen were written by David plus Psalms 68, 69, and 70. Anonymous authors wrote Psalms 66, 67, and 71. Solomon wrote Psalm 72, but it is considered David's words when he was near death.

Ch. 42–43 Thirsty for God

Ch. 44 A song remembering how God helped in past times

Ch. 45 Compare with Hebrews 1:8–9

Ch. 46–48 The Lord Most High is awesome

Ch. 49 Inability of riches to be anything of eternal value

Ch. 50 God wants honest hearts, not sacrifices and ritual

Ch. 51 David repents of his adulterous affair with Bathsheba

Ch. 52 Compare with 1 Samuel 22

Ch. 53 Ungodly are arrogant

Ch. 54–55 David prays for deliverance from enemies

Ch. 56–57 Compare to 1 Samuel 21:10 and 1 Samuel 24:1–22.

Ch. 58–59 Wicked will be judged (see 1 Samuel 19:11–18)

Ch. 60–61 When God seems absent, we can still trust Him

Ch. 62–63 David has a very close relationship with God

Ch. 64 David asks for God's protection from the plots of his enemies

Ch. 65–67 God is awesome and deserves praise

Ch. 68 God is good and very powerful

Ch. 69 David is overwhelmed with negative emotions

Ch. 70–71 David places his life in God's hands, trusting only Him

Ch. 72 Solomon asks for wisdom to lead God's people, and God will bless them.

PEOPLE, PLACES, HAPPENINGS

What did David say to himself when he was depressed? (42:5, 11; 43:5)

Who knows our secrets? (44:21)

God is our refuge even though _____? (46:1–3)

Will we be able to take our riches with us when we die? (49:16–17)

What had God's people done that displeased Him? (50:16–20)

Who did David sin against? (51:4)

What does David implore God to do for him? (51:7, 11)

What does God look for in our heart(character)? (51:17)

Who is a fool? (53:1)

In Psalm 56, what did David repeat? (56:4, 10–11)

How far do God's mercy and truth reach? (57:10)

Even though Saul had David's house watched, what did David do? (59:16–17)

What phrase did David repeat in Psalm 62? (62:1–2, 5–6)

What awaits those who allow God to refine them as silver? (66:10, 12)

Praise Him who does what? (68:4)

God is a father to the _____, and a defender of _____. (68:5)

How did David feel at the beginning of Psalm 69? (69:1–4)

David asked of God that those who seek Him not be _____ or _____ because of David's sins. (69:6)

Compare 69:20–21 with Matthew 27:48 and John 19:28–30. Who are these two verses talking about?

How long had David trusted God? (71:5)

How much will David praise God? (71:14–17)

What was David's desire? (71:18)

A NOTE FROM YOUR BIBLE STUDY MENTOR

A good portion of the third book of Psalms deals with Israel's history, downfall, and captivity.

Who is the happy person? What is God like? Is David always happy? Does he suffer at times from dark, despondent thoughts like most people?

PSALMS
Part 3: Book 3 • Psalms 73–89

LESSON
33

In Psalms Book 3, Psalms 73–83 were written by Asaph, a songwriter, arranger, and orchestra director under the rule of David and Solomon (1 Chronicles 15:16–17, 2 Chronicles 5:12). The sons of Korah wrote Psalms 84–85 and 87–88. Korah was a direct descendant of Levi's son, Kohath, and a leader of worship. Levi was the tribe set apart by God to be the priests of His people. David wrote Psalm 86. Psalm 89 was written by Ethan, the Ezrahite.

Ch. 73 Envying people who do not follow God, but are prosperous anyway

Ch. 74 A plea for help to the God who can do anything

Ch. 75 All of creation proves God is near

Ch. 76 God is the Almighty One

Ch. 77 A lamentation for an extended period without God's blessing

Ch. 78 A review of Israel's history and God's provision

Ch. 79 Destruction of Jerusalem

Ch. 80 Prayer that Israel will be restored

Ch. 81 God reminds His people of His deliverance, and of their unfaithfulness to Him

Ch. 82 God wants the poor, orphans, and needy to be cared for

Ch. 83 Prayer against their enemies

Ch. 84 Happy is the person who trusts in God

Ch. 85 People are brought back from captivity

Ch. 86 God is merciful and patient

Ch. 87 Praise for God's city

Ch. 88 A prayer from a dark place

Ch. 89 God's people were a blessed people, but now they have been forsaken

PEOPLE, PLACES, HAPPENINGS

How did the writer almost slip? (73:1–3)

When did he begin to understand? (73:17)

Who or what was most important to the psalmist? (73:25–26)

What is controlled by God? (74:16–17)

What did God command the fathers to do? (78:5)

Why were they to pass on their knowledge to their children? (78:6–8)

Why was God angry with them? (78:22)

What kind of food was manna? (78:24–25)

How were God's people hypocritical? (78:36–37)

Compare Psalm 79 to 2 Chronicles 36:15–19. What was happening?

What does the psalmist repeat three times? (80:3, 7, 19)

What is Israel compared to? (80:8; Isaiah 5:1, 7)

Did the people want God? (81:11)

What does God long for? (81:13)

What is the desired effect of the destruction of their enemies? (83:18)

What should they be careful not to do? (85:8)

Is God reluctant to forgive? (86:5)

What does David pray? (86:11–12; Deuteronomy 6:5)

Describe God. (86:15)

What belongs to the Lord? (89:11)

God's theocracy is based on what? (89:14)

A NOTE FROM YOUR BIBLE STUDY MENTOR

In this next lesson, Psalms Book 4, you might make a list of the words that describe God. I would encourage you to keep that list in your Bible or wallet for the times when you experience doubt and fear.

PSALMS

Part 4: Book 4 • Psalms 90–106

In Psalms Book 4, Moses wrote Psalm 90, and David wrote Psalms 101 and 103. The remaining psalms were by anonymous writers.

Ch. 90 God is eternal

Ch. 91 God is our protector if we will live in Him

Ch. 92 It is good to give thanks to God

Ch. 93 God is everlasting

Ch. 94 The wicked are foolish

Ch. 95 A call to worship and faith (Compare 95:8–11 with Numbers 14:1–24 and Hebrews 3:7–12)

Ch. 96 Worship the Lord in humility

Ch. 97 God reigns over all

Ch. 98 Joyfully praise God

Ch. 99 God is holy (see 1 Peter 1:15–16 and Revelation 15:3–4)

Ch. 100 Call to worship

Ch. 101 David wants to rid himself of sin

Ch. 102 A cry for help to a God who lives forever

Ch. 103 The Lord is good, kind, and merciful

Ch. 104 God has made all the world and all in it

Ch. 105 Retelling of Israel's history from Joseph through the Exodus

Ch. 106 Further retelling of Israel's history

PEOPLE, PLACES, HAPPENINGS

How long has God existed? (90:2)

Why should we be aware of the length of our life? (90:12)

If we abide under God's wings, of what do we not need to be afraid? (91:5–6)

List the instruments used to praise God. (92:3)

What is the Lord mightier than? (93:3–4)

Does God see and hear everything? (94:8–11)

Why should people worship God? (95:3)

What are verses 95:8–11 referring to? (see Numbers 13:31 through 14:1–24)

What is glory? (96:7–8)

What is the foundation of God's throne? (97:2)

What in nature can praise God? (98:7–8)

God was what to Moses, Aaron, and Samuel? (99:8)

What are we to know/acknowledge? (100:3)

What two characteristics of God will last forever? (100:5)

How does the writer describe his situation? (102:6–7)

What will grow old and be thrown away like an old garment? (102:25–26)

List the benefits of God. (103:3–5)

Describe God. (103:8–10)

How great is God's mercy? (103:11)

How far are our sins removed from us? (103:12; Isaiah 43:25)

With what does God clothe Himself? (104:1–2)

How long will the psalmist worship God? (104:33)

What was Israel's downfall? (106:13)

A NOTE FROM YOUR BIBLE STUDY MENTOR

As you read the Psalms that David wrote, try to write down a description of what you learned about David's concept of God. Did he struggle with his faith? Did he find help? Did his struggles cause him to turn from God, or did they lead him to God?

Read his words in Lesson 35, Psalms Pt. 5. When life gets complicated, you might go to the Psalms and read what others wrote when they felt discouraged.

PSALMS

Part 5: Book 5 • Psalms 107–150

Book 5 of Psalms was written to encourage people to worship and praise God. David wrote Psalms 108–110, 122, 124, 131, 133, 138–145 and Solomon wrote Psalm 127. The remaining psalms were by anonymous writers.

Ch. 107 God's deliverance comes when people cry out to Him.

Ch. 108 David expressing his faith in God

Ch. 109 David asks for help from his enemies

Ch. 110 Foretelling of the Messiah

Ch. 111 Praise to the Lord

Ch. 112 Blessed is the one who fears the Lord

Ch. 113–114 Praise God for His kindness and deliverance

Ch. 115 Futility of idol worship

Ch. 116 Grateful to be spared death

Ch. 117–118 Encouragement to praise God

Ch. 119 Acrostic about God's marvelous truths

Ch. 120–134 Songs of Ascents

Ch. 135–136 God's fame and mercy will endure forever

Ch. 137–138 Longing for home and God's goodness

Ch. 139 God knows all about each person

Ch. 140–141 Prayer for deliverance from evil people and to keep himself from being evil

Ch. 142–143 A prayer for relief from persecutors

Ch. 144–145 Songs of praise written by David

Ch. 146–150 Songs of praise

PEOPLE, PLACES, HAPPENINGS

What phrases are repeated in 107:6, 13, 19, and 28?

What phrases are repeated in 107:8, 15, 21, and 31?

How far do God's mercy and truth reach? (108:4)

What words from 110:1, 4 are repeated in Hebrews 1:13 and 5:6?

What is the beginning of wisdom? (111:10)

Who is blessed? (112:1)

Describe idols. (115:4–7)

How many sections are in Psalm 119?

How many verses in each section of Psalm 119?

In Psalm 119, what terms represent the word of God? There are ten.

Does God want us to worry? (127:1–2)

Who would be able to stand before God if He always kept records of our iniquities? (130:3–4)

What phrase is repeated in Psalm 136?

Where can a person go where God is not? (139:7–12)

When does God first know about us? (139:13, 16)

How does David describe God? (145:8–9)

What in space praises God? (148:1–5)

What elements in nature praise God? (148:8)

What animals are to praise God? (148:7, 10)

Who are instructed to praise God? (148:11, 12)

How are we to worship? (149:1, 3)

What instruments are used in worship? (150:3–5)

A NOTE FROM YOUR BIBLE STUDY MENTOR

If God came to you in a dream and told you to ask for anything and He would give it to you, what would you ask for?

God came to young King Solomon and did that very thing. What did Solomon ask for? What was God's response? Read the wise sayings in Proverbs.

PROVERBS
Words of Wisdom

In the book of Proverbs, King Solomon shared his wisdom. King Solomon is considered the wisest person who ever lived. God appeared to Solomon in a dream at the beginning of his reign shortly after King David died and said, "Ask. What shall I give you?" (1 Kings 3:5) Solomon acknowledged God's mercy toward his father King David and realized the scope of responsibility placed on him to follow in his father's footsteps. This is part of what he answered. "Therefore give to Your servant an understanding heart to judge Your people, that I may discern between good and evil. For who is able to judge these great people of Yours?" (1 Kings 3:9) Read the complete narrative in 1 Kings chapter three.

Ch. 1–9 Solomon teaching his son wisdom

Ch. 10–22:16 Wise sayings of Solomon

Ch. 22:17—24:34 Wise sayings from other people of his day

Ch. 25–29 Wisdom of Solomon

Ch. 30 Wisdom of Agur, son of Jakeh

Ch. 31:1–9 Wisdom taught to King Lemuel by his mother

Ch. 31:10–31 Acrostic on the virtuous woman

PEOPLE, PLACES, HAPPENINGS

Who despises wisdom? (1:7)

What is Solomon's primary advice to his son? (3:5–6)

Who does the Lord correct? (3:11–12)

What should be two main goals? (4:5–7)

What is considered a snare? (6:1–2)

What brings wisdom and understanding? (9:10)

Who is a grief to his mother? (10:1)

What is an abomination to God? (11:1)

Who is foolish and who is wise? (12:15)

The end of what is death? (14:12)

A fool despises what? (15:5)

What is better than a good dinner with hatred? (15:17)

What is better than silver or gold? (16:16)

Who is stronger than an army? (16:32)

Who is a grief to his father? (17:25)

What is in the power of the tongue? (18:21)

If a person wants friends, what must he do? (18:24)

What is a precious jewel? (20:15)

When is it better to live in the wilderness? (21:19)

Who keeps his soul from trouble? (21:23)

What is better than riches? (22:1)

What do the rich and poor have in common? (22:2)

How is being drunk described? (23:31–35)

Will we be held accountable for what we do? (24:12)

What is like apples of gold? (25:11)

How should we treat an enemy? (25:21–22; Romans 12:17–21)

What is gossip like? (26:22)

Why shouldn't we boast about tomorrow? (27:1)

Whose prayer is an abomination? (28:9; Isaiah 59:2)

When do the people of a nation rejoice, and when do they groan? (29:2)

How important is a virtuous wife? (31:10)

A NOTE FROM YOUR BIBLE STUDY MENTOR

What do you think of King Solomon and his wisdom? Do you know anyone who is so rich they have everything they could want? I don't.

King Solomon had everything. He had land, money, and women. Did that make him happy? Find out in the book of Ecclesiastes. He even wrote or had someone write a play called "The "Song of Solomon" about his love affair with a beautiful young girl. And yet, after having everything, what did he say is important?

ECCLESIASTES/SONG OF SOLOMON
All is Vanity/Romance

ECCLESIASTES
All is Vanity

In his later life, King Solomon wrote Ecclesiastes. He had been blessed with great success and riches. He had also wandered from his God. As he looked back over his life, he could see that nothing mattered except serving God.

Ch. 1 Life is the same

Ch. 2 Even extreme prosperity is empty

Ch. 3 A time for everything

Ch. 4 Friends are good

Ch. 5 Fear God; riches to the rich are vanity

Ch. 6 Sometimes family will go, leaving you with only your possessions

Ch. 7 He who fears God will escape some traps

Ch. 8 Obey the king because of your oath to God

Ch. 9 Life is simple; enjoy what you have

Ch. 10 No one is exempt from calamity

Ch. 11 Youth passes quickly, learn right ways early

Ch. 12 Follow God so that when you die your spirit returns to Him

---

PEOPLE, PLACES, HAPPENINGS

What is vanity like? (2:11, 17, 26; 4:4, 16; 6:9)

What happens to everyone? (2:16)

What is his simple advice for everyone? (3:12–13, 22)

Who is better than a foolish old king? (4:13)

What should you do about making vows to God? (5:1–5)

Does life happen to all, the good and the evil? (9:2–3)

What should be heard? (9:17)

Since God will bring all to judgment, what should we do? (11:10)

What is the conclusion of his musings? (12:13–14)

SONG OF SOLOMON
Romance

Song of Solomon is a story of love between Solomon and one of his concubines. It is a dialog between Solomon, the Shulamite woman, her friends, his friends, and her brothers.

Ch. 1 Physical appearance

Ch. 2 He calls to her

Ch. 3 Troubled night

Ch. 4 His thoughts of her

Ch. 5 He knocks, but she doesn't answer

Ch. 6–7 Appearances described

Ch. 8 Conversation between her and her brothers

PEOPLE, PLACES, HAPPENINGS

Why did she get tanned? (1:6)

To what does she compare her beloved? (2:9)

What time of day does she go looking for him? (3:1–3)

Did she answer him when he knocked on her door? (5:1–6)

Can anything quench true love? (8:7)

A NOTE FROM YOUR BIBLE STUDY MENTOR

Now you will begin studying the New Testament, starting with the Gospels that are told by four different men.

Matthew writes with the Jew in mind and what they would relate to. This lesson includes direct teaching and teaching using stories. It begins with the birth of Jesus and His cousin, John the Baptist. Did you know they were related?

MATTHEW
Part 1: The Messiah Comes

This gospel was written by Matthew, the disciple of Jesus who was also called Levi. During this time, the Jews were hoping for a Messiah that would come to overthrow their Roman rulers and restore Israel to its former glory. They did not understand Jesus came to bring a kingdom of the heart.

Ch. 1 Birth of Jesus

Ch. 2 His childhood

Ch. 3 Baptized by John the Baptist

Ch. 4 Temptation in the wilderness

Ch. 5–7 Sermon on the Mount

Ch. 8 Jesus demonstrates His power in various ways

Ch. 9 Forgiveness and fasting

Ch. 10 Twelve disciples called

Ch. 11 John Baptist

Ch. 12 Healing on Sabbath; Pharisees question authority of Jesus

Ch. 13 Parables

Ch. 14 John the Baptist killed; miracles over nature

PEOPLE, PLACES, HAPPENINGS

Why was He called Jesus? (1:21)

What prophecy was quoted in 2:6? (see Micah 5:2)

After His family returned from Egypt, where did they settle? (2:23)

What was the attitude of John the Baptist when Jesus wanted to be baptized by him? (3:14)

What happened when Jesus came out of the water? (3:16–17)

How long did Jesus fast in the wilderness? (4:1–2)

What did He quote to Satan? (4:4, 7, 10; Deuteronomy 6:16; 8:3; 10:20)

Who were the four fishermen He called to follow Him? (4:18–22)

How are we to treat our enemies? (5:43–48)

What indicates a person's priorities? (6:21)

What does 7:12 say?

Will many find the way that leads to life? (7:13–14)

Does doing amazing religious acts guarantee entrance into heaven? (7:21–23)

How was His teaching different from the teaching of the religious leaders of the day? (7:28–29)

What miracle of nature did Jesus perform? (8:23–27)

Why do you think the people of Gergesenes wanted Jesus to leave? (8:28–34)

Why did Jesus come? (9:9–13)

List the twelve disciples. (10:1–4)

Why would they be hated? (10:22)

Did Jesus come to bring peace? (10:34–39)

Where can true rest be found? (11:28–30)

What were the Pharisees concerned about? (12:9–14)

Why couldn't the majority understand the teachings of Jesus? (13:14–15)

List the common items compared to the kingdom of heaven. (13:24, 31, 33, 44, 45, 47)

What happened to John the Baptist? (14:1–12)

Why couldn't Peter keep walking on water? (14:30–31)

A NOTE FROM YOUR BIBLE STUDY MENTOR

By the second part of Matthew, Jesus had many followers. They were amazed at seeing sight restored to blind people, the dead raised, and food multiplied before their eyes.

When Jesus rode a donkey into Jerusalem, His fans went ahead cheering and laying palm branches in front of Him like He was their hero. Where were these fans a few days later?

MATTHEW

Part 2: Messiah's Passion

The remainder of Matthew's Gospel records more of Jesus' teachings, as well as, His arrest, hasty trial, crucifixion, and death on the cross.

Ch. 15 Outward religious life might hide inner sin

Ch. 16 Religious leaders want a sign

Ch. 17 Three disciples witness the Transfiguration of Jesus

Ch. 18 Kingdom success is the opposite of secular success

Ch. 19 Marriage and divorce

Ch. 20 God's reward is the same for all

Ch. 21 Palm Sunday events

Ch. 22 Resurrection is discussed

Ch. 23 Jesus exposes the Pharisees and scribes

Ch. 24 Signs of the last days

Ch. 25 Jesus describes His return to earth

Ch. 26 Last Supper, Jesus arrested

Ch. 27 Trial of Jesus, crucifixion, and burial

Ch. 28 His resurrection

PEOPLE, PLACES, HAPPENINGS

Why were the Pharisees upset? (15:2)

What was the response from Jesus? (15:3–6)

Who did the people say Jesus might be? (16:14)

From that time, what did Jesus begin to show His disciples? (16:21; 17:22, 23; 20:17–19)

What did the voice in the clouds say? (17:5)

What should we do when someone sins against us? (18:15–17; Luke 17:3–4)

How many times are we to forgive the same person? (18:21–22)

What did Jesus say about marriage and divorce? (19:4–9)

Which of the two sons did what his father asked? (21:28–32)

What happened to the man who came to the wedding feast without a wedding garment? (22:11–13)

What three titles are His followers not to be called? (23:8–10)

Who is the greatest? (23:11)

What did Jesus call the scribes and Pharisees? (23:25, 27, 29)

After the great tribulation, what will happen? (24:29)

What will life be like preceding His return? (24:38–39)

Who was the everlasting fire prepared for? (25:41)

Why wasn't Jesus arrested during the feast? (26:5)

Who betrayed Jesus? (26:14–16)

How could Jesus have prevented His arrest? (26:53)

What happened after Peter denied knowing Christ three times? (26:69–75)

What became of Judas? (27:3–5)

What was torn in two pieces from top to bottom when Jesus died? (27:51; Exodus 26:31–33)

Who bribed the guards? (28:11–15)

A NOTE FROM YOUR BIBLE STUDY MENTOR

Action! That's what describes Mark's account. Not so much teaching or parables. Enjoy studying this action–packed account of the life of Jesus.

MARK
Messiah's Ministry

The Gospel of Mark is an action–packed, historical account of Jesus Christ's ministry by a young man called John Mark. He traveled with Peter and Paul, and later with his cousin, Barnabas (Colossians 4:10). Read more about him in Acts 12 and 15.

Ch. 1 Jesus begins His ministry

Ch. 2 The authority of Jesus

Ch. 3 The twelve are called

Ch. 4 Parables

Ch. 5 His authority over demons

Ch. 6 Is this not the carpenter's son?

Ch. 7 Rituals do not clean the inside

Ch. 8 Pharisees begin to confront Him

Ch. 9 Transfiguration

Ch. 10 Following Jesus is more than keeping the commandments

Ch. 11 Righteous anger

Ch. 12 Pharisees question Jesus

Ch. 13 Signs of the end times

Ch. 14 Jesus celebrates the Passover and is arrested

Ch. 15 Crucifixion

Ch. 16 Resurrection

PEOPLE, PLACES, HAPPENINGS

What did the demons say about Jesus? (1:24)

What was the reaction of the scribes when Jesus forgave the young man his sins? (2:7)

Why was the Sabbath made? (2:27)

Who did Jesus consider to be His true family? (3:35)

In the parable of the Sower, what are the thorns? (4:19)

When the people saw the demon–possessed man sitting in his right mind, what did they want Jesus to do? (5:15–17)

How did Jesus know that someone with faith had touched Him? (5:21–30)

Who did King Herod think Jesus was? (6:14)

What was the disciples' reaction to Jesus calming the storms? (6:51; 4:41)

Do dishes not ceremoniously washed defile a person? (7:17–23)

Did the people keep quiet about what Jesus had done for them? (7:31–37)

Describe the apparent contradiction in 8:34–35.

What was the response of Jesus to the man whose son was having a convulsion? (9:23)

What was the man's response to Jesus? (9:24)

Why did Jesus, the Son of Man, come? (10:45)

What were the scribes and chief priests afraid of when Jesus overturned the tables? (11:18)

Whom did they fear in 12:12? Why?

What was the warning Jesus gave His disciples about the end times? (13:35–37)

Who mistreated Jesus at His trial? (14:53–65)

Who convinced Pilate to have Jesus crucified? (15:11–15)

What time of day did it get dark? (15:33)

After Jesus had finished speaking to His disciples, He ascended and sat down where? (16:19)

A NOTE FROM YOUR BIBLE STUDY MENTOR

In Luke, you will read about the angel Gabriel again. This time he spoke to a priest named Zacharias. He gave him such a startling message that Zacharias had a difficult time believing it. What happened to him because of his unbelief?

Did the ministry of John the Baptist conflict with the ministry of Jesus? What was the attitude of John the Baptist?

What did Peter, James, and John see on the mountain that caused them to want to build three tabernacles? Did they enter a cloud that was at ground level? What did they hear?

LUKE

Part 1: Jesus—Son of Man

Luke, a physician and close friend of Apostle Paul, wrote his account of the life of Jesus from a historical point of view. He wanted to give Theophilus an accurate account of the life and ministry of the Son of Man, the Savior.

Ch. 1 Birth of John the Baptist
Ch. 2 Birth of Jesus
Ch. 3 Ministry of John the Baptist
Ch. 4 Temptation of Jesus
Ch. 5 Forgiveness and healing
Ch. 6 Jesus is Lord of the Sabbath
Ch. 7 Amazing faith
Ch. 8 Power over nature and demons
Ch. 9 Transfiguration
Ch. 10 Seventy people sent out to preach and heal
Ch. 11 Jesus teaches

PEOPLE, PLACES, HAPPENINGS

What was Mary's response to Gabriel's message? (1:38)

What happened after Zacharias wrote down John's name? (1:63–64)

How did Simeon happen to be in the temple when Mary and Joseph brought their required offering after the birth of Jesus? (2:25–32)

What was Jesus' response to His parents when they found Him in the temple? (2:49)

How did John the Baptist speak of Jesus? (3:16)

Which of Noah's three sons is in the ancestry of Jesus? (3:36)

How extensive was the temptation of Jesus in chapter 4? (Hebrews 4:15)

What was Jesus like when He came back from His forty days of temptation? (4:14)

Using Leviticus 14:1–20, briefly describe the procedure for a leper to be pronounced clean by the priest. (5:12–14)

What was the Pharisees' opinion of the tax collectors? (5:27–30)

How are we to be like God? (6:35–36)

What is the person compared to who hears the words of Jesus and does them? (6:46–49)

For the healing of his servant, what did the centurion want Jesus to do? (7:1–7)

What did Jesus reply? (7:9)

Who loves Jesus the most? (7:41–47)

When Jesus calmed the storm, how did the disciples react? (8:25)

Were the people who knew of the demon-possessed man happy with Jesus? (8:35–37)

Describe the transfiguration of Jesus. (9:27–36)

When the 70 people returned to Jesus, what was to concern them? (10:17–20)

What was the reaction of the scribes and Pharisees to Jesus' teachings? (11:53–54)

A NOTE FROM YOUR BIBLE STUDY MENTOR

Jesus upset the church of His day by confronting the leaders. Why? What had they done wrong? He also revealed a little of what it will be like in the end times, and gave clues in the next lesson to look for as that time gets close.

He explained the kingdom of God and the principles that rule it. If a person belongs to that kingdom, how will they be different from someone who does not belong to it?

LUKE

Part 2: Son of Man Fulfills His Purpose

In the second part of Luke, Jesus continued His explanation of kingdom of heaven principles, as the religious leaders of His day attempted to undermine His teachings. The Pharisees felt threatened because throngs of people were following Him.

Ch. 12 Jesus teaches

Ch. 13 Various parables

Ch. 14 Humility taught

Ch. 15 Parables of the lost

Ch. 16 Rich and poor

Ch. 17 The Kingdom of God

Ch. 18 Kingdom principles

Ch. 19 Jesus goes to Jerusalem for the Passover

Ch. 20 Jesus confronts the scribes, Pharisees, and Sadducees

Ch. 21 Signs of the end times

Ch. 22 Last Supper and Jesus' arrest

Ch. 23 Trial and Crucifixion of Jesus

Ch. 24 Resurrection and Ascension

PEOPLE, PLACES, HAPPENINGS

What is the lesson of the Parable of the Rich Fool? (12:20–21)

Did Jesus come to give peace? (12:51–53)

To what did Jesus compare Herod? (13:32)

List one instance when there is joy in heaven. (15:10)

Why was not one of the dead sent back to warn them? (16:31)

How many of the ten lepers came back to thank Jesus? (17:15–16)

What will life be like preceding the return of Jesus? (17:26–30)

What question did Jesus ask in 18:8?

Which man, Pharisee or tax collector, will be justified? (18:9–14)

What was Jesus predicting as He looked over the city of Jerusalem? (19:41–44)

In the Parable of the Vinedressers, how many servants were sent? (20:9–12)

What happened to the son that was sent after the servants were mistreated? (20:13–15)

Why were the chief priests and scribes so angry with Jesus? (20:19)

What was the opinion of some of the scribes about Jesus? (20:39)

When will we know the desolation is near? (21:20)

What warning did He give about being ready? (21:34)

Did His disciples find the room ready for Passover? (22:12–13)

What did Jesus do to the man's ear that was cut off? (22:51)

Why was Herod glad to have Jesus brought before him? (23:8)

After the meeting, how did Herod treat Jesus? (23:11)

Did the disciples believe the women's report of Jesus' resurrection? (24:11)

Jesus told His disciples what happened to Him was to fulfill what writings? (24:44)

A NOTE FROM YOUR BIBLE STUDY MENTOR

In the next lesson, John Pt. 1, Jesus began to reveal more about Himself—who He was and why He came. One evening, He met with a religious leader who requested a secret meeting. The leader was intrigued by this young man Jesus and wanted to know more.

Again, Jesus had many followers who looked to Him for miracles. He tried to teach them what His Father instructed Him to teach. Not everyone liked what they heard, and He nearly got stoned for some of His statements.

JOHN

Part 1: Jesus, the I Am

In this book, John highlighted the various titles Jesus gave Himself. Jesus used the first of several "I Am" titles in chapter six. He used these terms to help relate who He was to His followers. In chapter eight, He nearly got Himself stoned for using the simple title "I Am."

Ch. 1 Jesus was with the Father before the beginning of time

Ch. 2 He begins His ministry

Ch. 3 Jesus explains new birth to Nicodemus, a religious leader

Ch. 4 Samaritans welcome Jesus

Ch. 5 Healing on the Sabbath causes trouble for Jesus

Ch. 6 Jesus is the bread of life

Ch. 7 Jesus teaches at the feast

Ch. 8 The "I Am" is the light of the world

Ch. 9 Blind man healed proving Jesus deity

PEOPLE, PLACES, HAPPENINGS

What prophecy from Isaiah 40:3 did John the Baptist quote? (1:23)

What did John the Baptist call Jesus? (1:29)

What happened to the water in the large pots? (2:9–10)

What temple was Jesus talking about? (2:19–22)

Who was Nicodemus? (3:1)

What did Jesus tell Nicodemus was necessary to see the kingdom of God? (3:5–7)

How strong a belief was Jesus talking about? (3:14–15; Numbers 21:4–9)

How did John the Baptist view his future with Jesus? (3:30)

How many husbands had the Samaritan woman had in her lifetime? (4:18)

How many days did Jesus stay at Sychar? (4:40)

What was the second sign Jesus performed? (4:46–54)

Which of the Pharisees' laws did the healed man break? (5:9–10)

Why were the Pharisees so angry they wanted to kill Jesus? (5:18)

What was the work of God for them to do? (6:29)

Jesus said, "I am _____." (6:35)

When Jesus asked the disciples if they wanted to leave Him like many others, what did Peter say? (6:66–69)

Did Jesus' siblings believe in Him? (7:1–5)

What did people think of Jesus when He claimed there were people wanting to kill Him? (7:20)

What were the rivers of living water Jesus talked about? (7:38–39)

Jesus said, " I am _____." (8:12)
Who will walk in the light? (8:12)

Who will know the truth and be made free? (8:31–32)

What serious offense did Jesus commit that caused the Jews to try to stone Him? (8:58–59; Exodus 3:14)

What upset the Pharisees about the healing of the blind man? (9:13–16)

A NOTE FROM YOUR BIBLE STUDY MENTOR

As you read what Jesus said about Himself in the second lesson of John, consider your ideas about Him and what you have been taught. Are they the same? Is your concept of Jesus the same as you read in the Bible?

How does the Lord's prayer in Matthew compare to His prayer in the book of John?

JOHN
Part 2: The True Shepherd

In the second part of the Gospel of John, Jesus devoted time to explain how He was the true, good shepherd who cared for His sheep. This close relationship would mark the difference between His disciples and all other disciples. They would be so like Him that they would be treated as He was, but they were not to worry for He promised them an abundant life with the Holy Spirit being their teacher when He was gone.

Ch. 10 Good Shepherd

Ch. 11 Raising of Lazarus

Ch. 12 Jesus speaks of His death

Ch. 13 A new commandment

Ch. 14 Jesus, the Way

Ch. 15 Jesus is the Vine

Ch. 16 Another Helper will come after Jesus leaves

Ch. 17 Prayer of Jesus

Ch. 18 Arrest of Jesus

Ch. 19 Crucifixion (compare Psalms 22:16–18; Zechariah 12:10)

Ch. 20 Resurrection

Ch. 21 Jesus speaks to His disciples before He ascends to heaven

PEOPLE, PLACES, HAPPENINGS

Why do the sheep follow their shepherd? (10:4)

Who are the other sheep? (10:16; Luke 2:32; Isaiah 56:8; Ephesians 2:11–18)

How did Jesus explain that crucifixion was not forced on Him? (10:15, 17, 18)

How long had Lazarus been dead when Jesus finally arrived at Bethany? (11:17, 39)

How do we know there were spies in the crowd that day? (11:45–48, 53)

Why did Jesus come to earth? (12:27; 10:17–18)

Compare 12:32 with Numbers 21:8. How would Jesus die?

Were there believers among the rulers? (12:42–43)

What did Jesus reveal to His disciples at the Passover dinner? (13:21)

What was the new commandment? (13:34)

How were they to love each other? (13:34; 15:12)

Did Jesus say there was more than one way to the Father? (14:6)

What will happen to the one who loves Jesus Christ? (14:21, 23)

Jesus said, "I am _____." List them. (10:7; 10:11; 11:25; 14:6; 15:1)

Why did Jesus explain the essential relationship of the branch to the vine? (15:11)

Why would His followers be hated? (15:18–19)

Who was the Helper that would come after Jesus ascended to heaven? (15:26; 16:7, 13)

How did Jesus send out His disciples? (17:18)

Why was it important that there be perfect unity? (17:21, 23)

What happened to the soldiers when Jesus answered, "I am He"? (18:6)

Who were Caiaphas and Annas? (18:13)

How did Pilate feel about condemning Jesus to death? (19:7–8)

Were the chief priests agreeable to the sign Pilate put above Jesus? (19:19–22)

How many days passed after the resurrection before Thomas saw Jesus? (20:21–28)

A NOTE FROM YOUR BIBLE STUDY MENTOR

Jesus had gone back to heaven and left His disciples to be witnesses of Him. The Book of Acts recorded the birth of the church. The early church drew lots of attention and grew rapidly, but was it well received by the Jewish church leaders?

It seemed the average person on the street watched with amazement but thought carefully before joining them. I wonder why?

ACTS
Part 1: Birth of Christianity

At the beginning of the book of Acts, before Jesus Christ ascended into heaven, He instructed His followers to wait in Jerusalem to be baptized with the Holy Spirit. This baptism would empower the believers, and they would be His witnesses. This was the birth of Christianity. Luke, the physician, was the author of this book. Compare Luke 1:1–4 with Acts 1:1–3.

Ch. 1 Instructions to wait in Jerusalem

Ch. 2 Holy Spirit comes on the day of Pentecost (see Leviticus 23:15)

Ch. 3 Crippled man healed, the beginning of a ministry

Ch. 4 Peter and John arrested by church leaders

Ch. 5 Group of apostles arrested

Ch. 6 Delegating the work

Ch. 7 Stephen's sermon

Ch. 8 Philip preaches

Ch. 9 Saul's conversion

Ch. 10 Cornelius summons Peter to Caesarea

Ch. 11 Peter explains his taking the gospel to Gentiles

Ch. 12 Peter in prison

Ch. 13 Paul's first missionary journey

Ch. 14 His journey continues throughout Asia Minor (Turkey)

PEOPLE, PLACES, HAPPENINGS

What was Jesus' promise to the apostles if they would wait in Jerusalem? (1:8)

What did the men in white apparel tell the followers as they stared into the sky? (1:10–11)

List the three supernatural manifestations of the coming of the Holy Spirit in the upper room. (2:2–4)

What did Peter and John do for the lame man? (3:6–7)

What healed the man? (3:16)

What was the heart of their message? (4:12)

What did the followers do after hearing of their arrest? (4:24–30)

Why did Ananias and Sapphira die? (5:2, 4, 9)

What was Gamaliel's advice? (5:33–39)

Describe Stephen. (6:8)

What was the reaction to his sermon? (7:54–60)

Who was standing nearby? (7:58)

What was Saul doing to the believers? (8:3)

What was the sorcerer's sin? (8:20)

What happened to Philip after baptizing the eunuch? (8:39–40)

How long was Saul blind? (9:9)

What was Ananias' reaction to the Lord's instruction in his vision? (9:13–14)

How did the disciples in Jerusalem receive Saul? (9:26)

What was the meaning of Peter's vision? (10:9–16, 28–29, 44–45)

Where were the disciples first called Christians? (11:26)

What happened to Herod? (12:23)

Where did Saul begin to be called Paul? (13:4–6, 9)

What did Paul and Barnabas do when they were expelled from Antioch? (13:51)

What happened to Paul at Lystra? (14:19–20)

A NOTE FROM YOUR BIBLE STUDY MENTOR

This is a big day! You are now three-fourths of the way through this study of the Bible. Awesome! You have accomplished much. I hope you are as proud of you as I am.

Lots of action was recorded in the remainder of this book of Acts. There was trouble between Paul and Barnabas. Paul and Silas got arrested for preaching and spent the night in jail. During the night, they were freed when an earthquake broke open the doors.

Apparently, Paul could be long-winded. A young man, sitting in an open window, fell asleep listening to Paul and fell out the third-floor window. What happened to him?

Riot in Ephesus. A plot to kill Paul. Paul was bitten by a deadly snake. Lots of action to keep you interested.

ACTS
Part 2: Paul and the Apostles Spread the Gospel

In the second part of the book of Acts, Christianity spread as the apostles traveled throughout the region carrying the message of repentance and baptism to both Jew and Gentile. Paul took a second and a third missionary trip with Silas, leaving Barnabas to take Mark with him.

Ch. 15 Essential Christian behavior for the Gentiles

Ch. 16 Silas joins Paul on his second missionary journey

Ch. 17 Paul and Silas rejected at Thessalonica

Ch. 18 Paul spends time in Corinth

Ch. 19 Riot in Ephesus

Ch. 20 Pastoral word to the disciples in Ephesus

Ch. 21 Paul's journey to Jerusalem

Ch. 22 Paul speaks from the top of the stairs

Ch. 23 Plot to kill Paul foiled

Ch. 24 Paul's defense before Felix

Ch. 25 Paul before Festus

Ch. 26 Paul's appeal to King Agrippa

Ch. 27 Paul's voyage to Rome

Ch. 28 Paul in Rome

PEOPLE, PLACES, HAPPENINGS

What was the disagreement between Jewish Christians and Gentile Christians? (15:1)

What was the decision? (15:28–29)

Why did the slave girl's master have Paul and Silas arrested? (16:16–19)

Did Paul and Silas escape after the earthquake? (16:25–28)

Who did Paul teach about? (17:23–25)

What was Paul's source of income, his occupation? (18:1–3)

How long was Paul at Corinth? (18:11)

His second journey ended at _____. (18:19, 22)

What happened to the seven sons of Sceva? (19:13–16)

What caused the riot in Ephesus? (19:23–27)

Why were the believers sad when Paul left for Jerusalem? (20:38)

Describe the prophecy by Agabus about Paul. (21:10–11)

Why were the people angry with Paul? (21:28)

Where did the garrison commander take Paul? (21:34)

Why did the commander need to be careful how he handled Paul as a prisoner? (22:25–29)

What was the conspiracy against Paul? (23:15)

How was their plan foiled? (23:16–24)

How long was Paul kept at Herod's Praetorium? (23:35; 24:27)

Did Festus pronounce judgment on Paul? (25:12)

Why did Festus want King Agrippa to hear Paul? (25:25–27)

Before he became a believer, how had Paul treated the Christians? (26:10–11)

Why had the Jews tried to kill Paul? (26:19–21)

What kept Paul from being set free? (26:32)

How long had they endured stormy weather on the trip to Rome? (27:27)

What happened to Paul that caused the local people to first think he was a murderer, then that he was a god? (28:3–6)

A NOTE FROM YOUR BIBLE STUDY MENTOR

As you study the letter to the Romans, you will get a clear picture of what faith in Christ means.

Is there any person good enough to go to heaven?

If you are a believer, do you struggle to live right? Don't think you are alone. Even Paul despaired of getting it right. Apostle Paul? Yes, Paul. Did he find freedom from the tendency to sin? Will sin have dominion over us? What can be done?

Can anything be done? Has it already been done? What about the words "know" and "reckon"?

ROMANS
Part 1: Explanation of Christianity

In this book, Paul wrote to the believers in Rome to explain that only God was righteous and that all people have sinned. He told them it was only faith in the death of Christ that justified a person, not obeying the law or doing good works.

Ch. 1 Man's unrighteousness

Ch. 2 God's righteousness

Ch. 3 All have sinned, Jews and Gentiles

Ch. 4 Justification is through faith, not keeping the law

Ch. 5 Jesus Christ's death provides the gift of salvation

Ch. 6 We died with Christ and are free from the power of sin

Ch. 7 The law of sin fights against the new life

Ch. 8 Holy Spirit provides the ability to be free from the power of sin

PEOPLE, PLACES, HAPPENINGS

What is Paul's theme of this letter to the Roman church? (1:16–17)

List two reasons prompting God to give them over to their sinful lives. (1:21)

What third sin did they commit? (1:28)

What leads to repentance? (2:4)

How do we know God does not have favorites? (2:11)

What kind of hypocrisy was being demonstrated in the church? (2:21–23)

Can anyone be justified by keeping the law? (3:20)

How many people are sinners? (3:23)

How is man justified? (3:28)

If a person works to earn salvation, is it grace? (4:4)

Who is righteous? (4:5)

If keeping the law results in justification, what happens to faith? (4:14)

How do we obtain peace with God? (5:1)

How did God demonstrate His love for us? (5:8)

Through one man's righteous act what came to all? (5:18)

How can a person be free from sin? (6:5–6)

Are believers to remain under the dominion of sin? (6:14)

What are the wages of sin? (6:23)

How are believers free from the pull of a sinful nature? (7:6)

What is the conflict between the old nature and the new life? (7:15–17)

Who saves us from this predicament? (7:24–25)

If the old, carnal nature dominates, what happens? (8:6)

Who gives the ability to live righteously? (8:11)

Are believers obligated to live according to their old nature, to yield to temptation? (8:12–13)

A NOTE FROM YOUR BIBLE STUDY MENTOR

Jews versus Gentiles. Why did the Jews have trouble with the Gospel message? Are the Jews better than the Gentiles? Are the Gentiles better than the Jews?

In the local church group, are some people more important than others? Are some unimportant? Find answers to these and other questions in the second lesson of Romans.

Then finally, how does faith in Jesus Christ affect our daily lives?

ROMANS

Part 2: Living the Christian Life

In the second part of Romans, after Paul explained the theology of the Christian life to both the Jews and the Gentiles, he encouraged them to live it in their everyday lives.

Ch. 9 Israel stumbles over faith

Ch. 10 Israel needs to come to God by faith like everyone else

Ch. 11 Gentiles are not better than Jews; all is of grace

Ch. 12 Every believer has a vital role

Ch. 13 Respect those in authority

Ch. 14 There will be minor differences; do not let them become a problem

Ch. 15 With one mind and one mouth, glorify God

Ch. 16 Greetings sent to several friends

PEOPLE, PLACES, HAPPENINGS

Why did Israel fail to obtain righteousness? (9:32)

What did Israel do incorrectly? (10:3)

What needs to be done to be saved? (10:9)

Is there a distinction between Jew and Greek? Why? (10:12–13)

Can it be grace and works? (11:6)

How did Paul hope to win the Jews? (11:13–15)

Could the Gentiles boast of their faith? (11:17–18)

God's goodness continues toward the believing Gentile under what condition? (11:22)

Paul pled with them to do what? (12:2)

Is each believer in a group necessary? (12:4–5)

List some ways to behave like a Christian. (12:10–13)

Who gives governments their authority? (13:1)

Are we to pay taxes? (13:7)

Why is love the fulfillment of the law? (13:8–10)

How are believers to live? (13:13)

What kind of differences might there arise in a group of believers? (14:1–6)

What did Paul say about the judgment seat? (14:10–12)

How can a person's good deeds be spoken of as evil? (14:15–17)

What is one of the prophecies telling salvation was also for the Gentiles? (15:9–12; Isaiah 11:10; Isaiah 65:1)

Paul told the Roman believers that they would be able to do what? (15:14)

What does admonish mean?

Where did Paul hope to go after visiting with the believers in Rome? (15:28)

Why did Paul want them to pray fervently for him? (15:31–32)

Where did Phoebe live? (16:1; Acts 18:18)

Who were Aquila and Priscilla? (16:3; Acts 18:1–3)

How many house churches were there in Rome? (16:5, 10, 11, 14, 15)

A NOTE FROM YOUR BIBLE STUDY MENTOR

Do you know of a perfect church? I've heard it said that if you do find a perfect church, don't go to it because then it won't be perfect. No believer is perfect, but growth should be evident.

Each church, each group of believers, is made up of people in various stages of spiritual growth. Some are serious believers, and some are just attendees.

Paul wrote to the church in Corinth to help them with some trouble in the church. Do you have any idea what that trouble was?

1 CORINTHIANS

The Wisdom of God vs. Wisdom of Man

1 Corinthians was Paul's first of two recorded letters to the church in the city of Corinth, a city in Greece. He had heard some disturbing news concerning activities occurring in that body of believers. In this letter, he explained to them that this new way of life, which was not understood by the natural person, was based on the wisdom of God.

Ch. 1 All believers are united in Christ

Ch. 2 Wisdom of God

Ch. 3 Wisdom of world is foolishness with God

Ch. 4 Everything is for Christ

Ch. 5 Immorality in the church must be judged

Ch. 6 Prefer being cheated rather than cause trouble

Ch. 7 Marriage

Ch. 8 Believers should not use freedom at the risk of another's faith

Ch. 9 Paul does not insist on his rights for fear it will jeopardize the gospel message

Ch. 10 Give no offense, but rather do all for the glory of God

Ch. 11 Purpose of Lord's supper and right behavior

Ch. 12 Spiritual gifts

Ch. 13 Greatest is love

Ch. 14 Order in meetings

Ch. 15 Christ our resurrection hope

Ch. 16 Collection for the saints and Paul's plans

PEOPLE, PLACES, HAPPENINGS

How did Paul describe the message of the cross? (1:18)

How did Paul describe the effectiveness of the message? (2:4–5)

Why is it necessary to be born again to understand the things of God? (2:14; John 3:3)

How did Paul describe a believer as a temple of God? (3:16–17)

What is foolishness with God? (3:19)

Paul would come in person in one of two ways. Describe the two ways. (4:18–21)

Are believers to be separate and have nothing to do with unbelievers? (5:9–13)

Why shouldn't a believer take another believer to court? (6:1–6)

Do believers have ownership over themselves? Why? (6:19–20)

A man or a woman believer who is unmarried is free to do what? (7:32–34)

When is a woman free to remarry? (7:39)

If a believer wounds another believer with his freedom, against whom does he sin? (8:9–13)

Believers are in a race to obtain what kind of crown? (9:25)

What did Paul say about temptation? (10:13)

Believers are to do all _____. (10:31)

What does taking the Lord's supper say? (11:26)

List the nine gifts of the spirit. (12:8–10)

Describe the necessity of each believer in the local body? (12:20–26)

Can having great faith, sacrificing their life, or giving all to charity be for nothing? (13:1–3)

Describe biblical love. (13:4–7)

Spiritual gifts are for what? (14:12)

Who are tongues a sign for? (14:22)

What did Paul receive that he passed on to the church in Corinth? (15:3–4)

Why was he the least of all the apostles? (15:9)

How were they to help the saints in Jerusalem? (16:1–2)

A NOTE FROM YOUR BIBLE STUDY MENTOR

Paul finds himself in the awkward position of having to defend his place as an apostle. Apparently, people have been talking about him. How does he deal with that situation in the second letter to the Corinthians? Is he proud? Does he seek to vindicate himself? What is important to him?

2 CORINTHIANS
Paul's Defense

In 2 Corinthians, Apostle Paul wrote again to the church in Corinth, this time in defense of his apostleship. Although he wasn't a very imposing person, and he used to persecute the church so that he considered himself the least of all the apostles, God had appointed him to be an apostle.

Ch. 1 Paul reports the trouble they had in Ephesus

Ch. 2 Welcome back the offender with forgiveness

Ch. 3 The message of the gospel is liberty in Christ

Ch. 4 Difficulties in ministering the gospel

Ch. 5 Ministry of reconciliation

Ch. 6 Unequally yoked

Ch. 7 Paul's previous letter brought sorrow that led to repentance

Ch. 8 Bring monetary gifts from Macedonia

Ch. 9 Cheerfully giving to those in Jerusalem

Ch. 10 Paul's spiritual authority is limited to what God has given him

Ch. 11 Paul reluctantly boasts

Ch. 12 Paul has seen heavenly visions

Ch. 13 Paul will visit them again

PEOPLE, PLACES, HAPPENINGS

What trouble did they have in Asia? (1:8; Acts 19:21–41)

How did they conduct themselves? (1:12)

Paul said that they preached the gospel with sincerity, not like some others who did what? (2:17)

The Spirit gives _____, the letter _____. (3:6)

Who blinds the minds of unbelievers? (4:4)

How had life been for Paul and Timothy? (1:1; 4:8–9)

Even though his physical body was wearing out, what was happening to his spirit? (4:16)

Describe a person in Christ. (5:17)

What is the ministry of reconciliation? (5:18–19)

List the troubles Paul and Timothy had. (6:4–10)

What did Paul warn the believers regarding relationships? (6:14–16)

What was Paul's defense? (7:2)

Describe the sorrow Paul was talking about? (7:8–9)

Does godly sorrow bring about a good result? (7:10)

Why did Paul remind them to have their monetary gifts ready when he came? (9:4)

What were some people saying about Paul? (10:10)

Who is approved? (10:18)

What did Paul tell about himself in his defense? (11:22–27)

How was Paul's thorn in the flesh described? (12:7)

Why did Paul take pleasure in rough times? (12:10)

Why will Paul mourn for some of the believers? (12:21)

This would be the _____visit. (13:1)

A NOTE FROM YOUR BIBLE STUDY MENTOR

The early church had its problems with doctrinal differences. Jewish Christian versus Gentile Christian? What did they do with their Jewish faith, traditions, and laws? Paul said it is only by faith in his letter to the Galatians.

Paul warned them that some were perverting the gospel by putting regulations on the believers. What was the problem?

Why is working for salvation wrong, cursed? Has Christ died in vain? When can His death not benefit us?

GALATIANS
Law vs. Grace

In the book of Galatians, Paul wrote to the church in Galatia when he heard of those who were trying to impose the Jewish law on the believers. In their confusion, they tried to combine law and grace.

Ch. 1 Turning away from the true gospel to another

Ch. 2 Grace is not achieved by fulfilling the demands of the law

Ch. 3 No one is justified by works

Ch. 4 Those who are believers are heirs of God through Jesus Christ

Ch. 5 Remain in the liberty of faith and grace

Ch. 6 As a body of believers, they need to take care of each other

PEOPLE, PLACES, HAPPENINGS

What amazed Paul about the believers in Galatia? (1:6–7)

What had the churches in Judea heard about Paul? (1:23)

Christ could have died in vain under what conditions? (2:21)

What was counted for Abraham as righteousness? (3:6)

Why is living by the law cursed? (3:10)

How is a believer Abraham's seed? (3:16, 29)

What distinction did Paul make in 4:9?

What were the names of Abraham's two sons? (4:22, 28; Genesis 16:1–16, 21:1–12)

If a believing Jew is circumcised, what happens to his faith? (5:2–3)

How does a believer keep from doing what is wrong? (5:16)

List the works of the flesh. (5:19–21) Check the dictionary for unfamiliar words.

List the fruits of the Spirit. (5:22–23)

Are the fruits the believer's efforts or from the Spirit? (5:22)

How are believers to treat those who fall and sin? (6:1)

What amounts to nothing? (6:15)

A NOTE FROM YOUR BIBLE STUDY MENTOR

Are you ready to find out who believers are in Christ Jesus? Paul's letter to the believers in Ephesus uses the words "in Him" multiple times.

If you are a believer, who are you? If you are a believer, how are you to (walk) live?

EPHESIANS
Who Are Believers in Christ?

In the book of Ephesians, Paul explained both Jew and Gentile believers were united by the death of Jesus Christ. Jesus Christ gave each believer an inheritance. All the blessings of Jesus Christ were theirs because they were placed in Him, through faith, by the Father.

Ch. 1 Redemption through the death of Jesus Christ

Ch. 2 Saved by grace, not works

Ch. 3 Mystery of joint heirs with Jesus Christ

Ch. 4 Turn away from the former life to live a new life in Christ

Ch. 5 Imitate God in daily life

Ch. 6 Family relationships

PEOPLE, PLACES, HAPPENINGS

What do believers have "in Him," Jesus Christ? (1:7)

Paul prayed that they will know what three things? (1:18–19)

What does God want to show in the ages to come? (2:7)

How did Jesus Christ bring peace between Jew and Gentile? (2:15–18)

List the four things Paul prayed the believers will have. (3:16–17)

What are the dimensions of God's love? (3:18)

Describe what Paul called childish believers. (4:14)

Describe the walk of the unbeliever. (4:17–19)

Why will the wrath of God come upon the world? (5:3–6)

How are believers to walk? (5:15–21)

What is the first commandment that is followed by a promise? (6:2; Deuteronomy 5:16; Exodus 20:12)

List the parts of the believer's armor. (6:14–17)

A NOTE FROM YOUR BIBLE STUDY MENTOR

If anyone had a right to brag about his accomplishments it would be Apostle Paul, but did he brag? What was his attitude? What was crucial to him? In his letter to the Philippians, Paul bared his soul as he awaited trial.

PHILIPPIANS
All For Christ

In Philippians, Paul emphasized the humility of Christ and urged the believers to be like Christ. Although Paul had much to brag about, he counted all his accomplishments as worthless compared to his walk with Jesus Christ. He encouraged them to take all their cares to the Lord in prayer, and the peace of God would sustain them.

Ch. 1 Paul lives entirely for Christ
Ch. 2 Let the humility of Christ be in the believer
Ch. 3 What Paul has accomplished is nothing compared to having Christ
Ch. 4 Paul's advice to his friends

PEOPLE, PLACES, HAPPENINGS

What was Paul confident about? (1:6)

What was Paul's conflict of interest? (1:21–24)

What did he hope to hear about their lives? (1:27)

What mind was Paul talking about? (2:5–8)

Who did Paul hope to send to them for a visit? (2:19)

What kind of relationship did Paul have with Timothy? (2:22)

If Paul wanted to brag, what could he brag about? (3:5–6)

Paul counted all things as loss compared to what? (3:8)

Did Paul dwell on the past? (3:13–14)

Who did Paul implore to be in agreement? (4:2)

What was his advice about worry? (4:6–7)

What did he encourage them to meditate on? (4:8)

A NOTE FROM YOUR BIBLE STUDY MENTOR

How much of Christian faith today is based on tradition? On what are believers to base their faith?

It seems the church at Colossae had mixed their faith with some traditions. In this letter to the Colossians, Paul encouraged them to see the preeminence of Christ and cautioned them to avoid falling back into legalism and tradition.

COLOSSIANS
Superiority of Christ

In Colossians, Paul wrote to the church at Colossae, encouraging them to set their minds on heavenly things. He emphasized the preeminence of Christ in all things. Their faith was based on what Christ had done for them and not on traditions.

Ch. 1 Christ is the image of the invisible God

Ch. 2 Relationship with Jesus Christ is more than mere philosophy

Ch. 3 Put off the old person and put on the new person

Ch. 4 Greetings from several people

PEOPLE, PLACES, HAPPENINGS

Who has qualified the believers to partake in this inheritance? (1:12)

What was created by Jesus Christ? (1:16)

How did Jesus Christ reconcile all to Himself? (1:19–20)

What was Paul's warning? (2:8)

What things have the appearance of wisdom? (2:16–23)

On what should the believer's mind be set? (3:1–2)

What are the believers to put off? (3:8)

What are the believers to put on? (3:10, 12)

What is to dominate or rule the heart of the believer? (3:15)

What was the church at Colossae to be vigilant in doing? (4:2)

Where was Paul while writing this letter? (4:3, 10, 18)

Who was bringing them news of Paul? (4:7–9)

A NOTE FROM YOUR BIBLE STUDY MENTOR

With technology, we have instant contact with friends and family. In Paul's time, letters or a person needed to be sent to get information. In the next lesson, he sent Timothy to see how the believers in Thessalonica were doing.

When Timothy returned was the news good or bad? Was Paul encouraged by their faith?

In the second letter, he encouraged the believers concerning the end times. What will the last days be like?

1 & 2 THESSALONIANS
Stay Strong In the Truth

Paul expressed relief at the news Timothy brought back after he sent him to visit the believers in the church at Thessalonica. In these letters, Paul encouraged the believers to live a life that would be a testimony to the unbelievers in their community.

1 THESSALONIANS
Stay strong

Ch. 1 Letter from Paul, Silvanus, and Timothy commends the believers for their good reputation

Ch. 2 They received the word because it was presented to them with integrity

Ch. 3 Paul is comforted by the news Timothy brought back from his visit with them

Ch. 4 Believers are to live an orderly life

Ch. 5 Closing instructions

PEOPLE, PLACES, HAPPENINGS

How did Paul open most of his letters? (1:1; Col. 1:1–2; Phil. 1:1–2; Eph. 1:1–2)

What is the reputation of the believers at Thessalonica? (1:7–10)

Paul and his fellow ministers had presented the gospel with integrity and not with what? (2:4–6)

Why had Paul sent Timothy to Thessalonica? (3:1–3)

What news did Timothy bring back to Paul and his friends? (3:6)

What did Paul urge them to do? (4:3–5, 11–12)

With what were they to comfort each other? (4:16–18)

What four things did Paul want them to do? (5:14)

2 THESSALONIANS
The Day of the Lord

Paul wrote to the believers about a time in the future when many will fall away from the faith.

Ch. 1 Paul is grateful they are thriving spiritually
Ch. 2 The Day of the Lord
Ch. 3 Warning against freeloading

PEOPLE, PLACES, HAPPENINGS

How will Jesus be revealed in the end? (1:7–8)

The Day of the Lord will not come until what happens? (2:3–4)

How will the lawless one be destroyed? (2:8)

Why will people perish? (2:10)

Who will guard the believers from the evil one? (3:3)

Did Paul expect free meals? (3:7–8; Acts 18:3)

A NOTE FROM YOUR BIBLE STUDY MENTOR

If you are a young person, never underestimate your influence. Paul was convinced that a young person, anointed by God, could be a good leader. He gave Timothy and Titus some real nuggets of wisdom that are still appropriate today for anyone in Christian leadership.

1 & 2 TIMOTHY/TITUS PHILEMON
Guard the Truth

1 TIMOTHY
Example of a Believer

Paul urged Timothy, in spite of his youth, to be an example of the believer

Ch. 1 Carefully guard the truth that he has received

Ch. 2 Instructions for men and women in the church

Ch. 3 Instructions for those who want to be an overseer

Ch. 4 Young Timothy is to be an example of the believer

Ch. 5 Paul's instructions to Timothy regarding how to treat others in the church

Ch. 6 Pursue the right things

PEOPLE, PLACES, HAPPENINGS

Where did Paul want Timothy to stay? (1:3)

Why did he want believers to pray for those in authority? (2:2)

Who is the mediator between God and man? (2:5)

What were the requirements for one who wanted to be a bishop? (3:2–7)

What were the requirements for one who desired to be a deacon? (3:8–12)

What will happen in later times? (4:1)

How was Timothy to treat the believers in the church? (5:1–2)

Who did Paul consider worse than an unbeliever? (5:8)

What is great gain? (6:6)

What is the root of all evil? (6:9–10)

2 TIMOTHY
Be strong in troubled times

Paul wrote to Timothy preparing him for difficult times

Ch. 1 Paul encouraged Timothy to stay true and not be ashamed of Paul's imprisonment

Ch. 2 Be strong and focused on the truth

Ch. 3 Perilous times are coming

Ch. 4 Preach, Timothy, preach

PEOPLE, PLACES, HAPPENINGS

Who were Timothy's mother and grandmother? (1:5)

Are believers to be fearful? (1:7)

Who frequently helped Paul? (1:16–17)

What must Timothy endure? (2:3)

What will the perilous times be like? (3:1–5)

Who will suffer persecution? (3:12)

What work was Timothy to do? (4:2, 5)

TITUS
Living Godly in the present age

Paul left Titus in Crete to set in order what was lacking in the local church.

Ch. 1 Qualifications for church elders
Ch. 2 Family relationships
Ch. 3 Recipients of grace have an obligation to live righteously

PEOPLE, PLACES, HAPPENINGS

Where did Paul leave Titus? (1:5)

Why were some teaching things they ought not? (1:11)

How should believers live? (2:11–12)

When should believers reject a divisive person? (3:10)

What were the believers of all ages to maintain? (2:7, 14; 3:1, 8, 14)

PHILEMON
Debt will be repaid

Paul sent Onesimus back to Philemon with a letter asking Philemon not to be too hard on Onesimus for running away. He had become a believer and had been helpful to Paul.

PEOPLE, PLACES, HAPPENINGS

How did Paul want Philemon to accept the returning runaway slave? (v. 15–16)

What did Paul want Philemon to charge to his account? (v. 18)

A NOTE FROM YOUR BIBLE STUDY MENTOR

Although the author of the book of Hebrews is unknown, you will find much treasure in its pages. It explains the new and better way. New and better than the Mosaic law that they had been living under for hundreds of years. How is what they now have better than what they had before?

HEBREWS

A Better Covenant

This letter to the Hebrew believers was written to explain to the Jewish community the truth of the gospel, the new and better covenant. Jesus Christ was the human expression of the Godhead, the final and perfect sacrifice, and the perfect priest who could understand them.

Ch. 1 God is revealed through His Son

Ch. 2 Through His death, the Son was made the perfect captain for all who believe in Him

Ch. 3 Comparison of sin and unbelief

Ch. 4 A rest is promised

Ch. 5 Christ, the High Priest who understands people

Ch. 6 Believers need to grow spiritually

Ch. 7 Temporary priest vs. eternal priest (see Genesis 14:18)

Ch. 8 New covenant replaces the old covenant

Ch. 9 Death of Christ established the new covenant

Ch. 10 Former sacrifices were a foreshadow of Christ's sacrificial death

Ch. 11 Faith hall of fame

Ch. 12 Individual believers are part of a great company

Ch. 13 Practical Christian advice for life

PEOPLE, PLACES, HAPPENINGS

How has God spoken to us? (1:2)

After He purged our sins, what did Jesus do? (1:3)

What did God say to the Son through a prophecy? (1:8; Psalm 45:6, 7)

Why was it necessary to give earnest heed to what they heard? (2:1)

Through His death, what did Jesus accomplish? (2:14)

What is the warning in 3:12?

Why did the word not profit them? (4:2)

Who has entered into the promised rest? (4:10)

Describe the word? (4:12)

Why is Jesus the High Priest who could sympathize with our weaknesses? (4:15)

What did Jesus learn? (5:8)

Is it possible for God to lie? (6:18)

Who did Abraham meet when he was returning from war? (7:1)

What did the name King of Salem mean? (7:2)

How did Levi receive tithes from Abraham? (7:9–10)

Because the priesthood of Jesus Christ continues forever, of what is He capable? (7:24–25)

What did the sacrifices of the priests serve? (8:5)

What was going to be different about the new covenant? (8:10)

What happened to the old covenant? (8:13)

How often did a priest go into the Most Holy Place? (9:7)

When Jesus went into the Most Holy Place, what did He bring? (9:12)

What can cleanse the conscience? Blood of animals or the blood of Jesus? (9:13–14)

What is necessary for remission? (9:22)

How often was Jesus offered? (9:28)

Did God desire sacrifices and burnt offerings? (10:8)

What does the veil represent? (10:20)

What is faith? (11:1)

List the ten people described in this chapter. (11:4, 5, 7, 8, 11, 20, 21, 22, 23, 31)

List some of the ways believers have been persecuted over the ages. (11:35–38)

How is the believer to run the race? (12:1–2)

Who does God chasten? (12:6)

If God does not chasten a person, what does that mean? (12:8)

How does the writer describe God? (12:29)

How does the writer describe Jesus? (13:8)

Where did this letter originate? (13:24)

A NOTE FROM YOUR BIBLE STUDY MENTOR

Two authors—James and Peter.

James wanted to see the evidence of their faith. What was he looking for?

Peter, how he changed from the impetuous disciple that denied knowing Christ after being His follower for three years! With strong faith, he encouraged the believers not to worry when life got difficult.

Doesn't sound like the same man to me. What about you?

JAMES/1 & 2 PETER
Active Faith

JAMES
Doers of the word

James wrote to the Jewish believers who had been through persecution and had moved to various places throughout the Roman world. He was concerned that their faith was evidenced by how they lived.

Ch. 1 The faith of a believer will be tested through various trials
Ch. 2 Faith is made evident through the life
Ch. 3 A person's speech is difficult to control
Ch. 4 Pride vs. humility
Ch. 5 Patiently continue in the faith

PEOPLE, PLACES, HAPPENINGS

What people did James write this letter to? (1:1)

Does God tempt people? (1:13–14)

What makes a person guilty of breaking all the law? (2:10)

Do demons believe in God? (2:19)

Who is a perfect person? (3:2)

How is the tongue described? (3:5, 6, 8–10)

How is friendship with the world described? (4:4)

If a believer knows to do good but doesn't do it, what is it? (4:17)

How effective were Elijah's prayers? (5:17–18)

1 PETER
Kept by the power of God

Peter wrote to believers who had moved throughout the Roman world to escape persecution. He encouraged them not to be concerned when life got complicated because God would be with them. He would keep them, perfect them, establish them and strengthen them.

Ch. 1 Rest your hope fully on grace as obedient children
Ch. 2 Have your conduct honorable before all people
Ch. 3 If you suffer for your faith in Christ, you are blessed
Ch. 4 Be serious, be watchful
Ch. 5 Cast all your care on God

PEOPLE, PLACES, HAPPENINGS

What is more precious than gold? (1:7)

What were the believers redeemed with? (1:18–19)

What is the effect of the chief cornerstone to a believer and an unbeliever? (2:6–8)

What are two titles for Jesus Christ? (2:25)

The eyes of the Lord are on whom? (3:12)

Why did Jesus Christ suffer? (3:18)

Should a believer be surprised when trials come their way? (4:12)

List the four things that God will do for the believer? (5:10)

2 PETER
There will be false teachers

Peter warned the believers to be aware of those who would distort the gospel and would try to convince people, through swelling words of emptiness, to follow them.

Ch. 1 Be diligent to make their calling sure
Ch. 2 False teachers
Ch. 3 Be diligent to be found in Christ

PEOPLE, PLACES, HAPPENINGS

The divine power of Jesus has given believers what? (1:3)

What was Peter talking about in 1:13–14? (see John 21:18)

What happened to the angels who sinned? (2:4)

What will the scoffers say in the last days? (3:3–4)

How will the day of the Lord come? (3:10)

What are the believers looking for? (3:13)

A NOTE FROM YOUR BIBLE STUDY MENTOR

The letters of John are short but vital. Ever wonder if you are a believer? John gives clues to let Christians know if they are true believers.

Jude was concerned about the condition of the church. Who had come into the church causing trouble?

1, 2, 3 JOHN/JUDE
True Believers

1 JOHN
Indications that we know God

He who is in the light, but does not act like it, is not a true believer. A true believer has the love of God in him. It was the new commandment made by Jesus when He was on earth.

Ch. 1 Fellowship with God

Ch. 2 How to know if we are in Him

Ch. 3 Difference between believers and non–believers

Ch. 4 John warns them to beware of false prophets

Ch. 5 John wrote so they would know they have eternal life

PEOPLE, PLACES, HAPPENINGS

What if believers say they are sinless? (1:8–10)

Is all lost with God if we sin? (2:1–2)

Who were the three groups of people John wrote to? (2:12–14)

What are the three things in the world that are not of God? (2:16)

Why was the Son of God manifested? (3:5, 8)

What is the commandment? (3:23)

Why test the spirits? (4:1)

How are the believers able to discern the spirit of truth from error? (4:6)

How was the love of God manifested(shown)? (4:9–10)

Why do believers love God? (4:19)

Who has eternal life? (5:12–13)

2 JOHN
Beware of deceivers

John wrote to encourage the believers to let the love of Christ be their goal and to beware of deceivers.

PEOPLE, PLACES, HAPPENINGS

What do the deceivers say? (v. 7)

Did John write all he wanted to say to them in this letter? (v. 12)

3 JOHN
Walk in truth

John wrote to Gaius to express his joy that he was walking in truth.

PEOPLE, PLACES, HAPPENINGS

What is John's greatest joy? (v. 4)

How does the ending of this letter compare with the end of 2 John? (v. 13–14)

JUDE
New and old apostates

Jude encouraged the believers to contend for the faith.

PEOPLE, PLACES, HAPPENINGS

What has happened in the church? (v. 4)

Describe the apostates. (v. 12–13)

Who can keep a believer from stumbling in their conduct? (v. 24)

A NOTE FROM YOUR BIBLE STUDY MENTOR

Congratulations! Only one remaining lesson. Can you believe it? You have accomplished what many people have only wished for. In this journey, you have gained a fundamental knowledge of the Bible.

Have you learned all there is to know from the Bible? No. There are depths of knowledge that are still waiting for you to discover.

I would encourage you to make Bible reading a regular part of your life. Each time you read you will learn more.

Now, to this last lesson—Revelation. You will read about 4 different colored horses, a dragon, 2 beasts, 2 men who lay dead for 3 days then come back to life, the new Jerusalem, and a new earth, plus much more.

REVELATION
Things to Come

Revelation is the record of the heavenly visions Apostle John received of things to come regarding the church, the unbelievers, and Israel during the end times. He had been exiled to the island of Patmos because of his faith.

Ch. 1 John receives revelations

Ch. 2 Messages to four churches

Ch. 3 Messages to three churches

Ch. 4 Throne in heaven

Ch. 5 Lamb and the scroll (see Isaiah 53:7)

Ch. 6 Opening six of the scrolls

Ch. 7 Those who are sealed by God

Ch. 8 Seventh Seal opened revealing seven angels with seven trumpets

Ch. 9 Fifth and sixth trumpet sounded

Ch. 10 Angel brings a little book

Ch. 11 Two prophets

Ch. 12 An enraged dragon

Ch. 13 Two beasts

Ch. 14 Proclamations from two groups of angels

Ch. 15 Seven angels, seven bowls

Ch. 16 Seven plagues/disasters

Ch. 17 Description of the woman, Babylon the Great

Ch. 18 The fall of the woman, Babylon the Great

Ch. 19 Battle against the King of Kings

Ch. 20 Satan bound one thousand years

Ch. 21 The New Jerusalem

Ch. 22 Conclusion of these visions to John

PEOPLE, PLACES, HAPPENINGS

Where was John at this time? (1:9)

List the four churches in chapter two and what they will receive if they overcome.

List the three churches in chapter three and what they will receive if they overcome.

Why is the Lord worthy to receive glory, honor, and power? (4:11)

What will worship the Lamb who was slain? (5:13)

What color were the horses? (6:2, 4, 5, 8)

Who were those in white robes? (7:9–14)

What happened immediately after the Lamb opened the seventh seal? (8:1)

Did people repent of their sins when they experienced the plagues? (9:20–21)

Was John allowed to write what the thunders said? (10:4)

What will happen to the two prophets? (11:3, 7–12)

Who was the dragon and how great was his influence? (12:9)

Who will worship the beast? (13:8; 17:8)

What did the 144,000 have on their forehead? (14:1)

After the bowls were given out, how long was it before anyone could enter the temple? (15:8)

Did people repent when they experienced God's wrath? (16:9, 11, 21)

What was the woman drunk with? (17:6)

How long did it take to destroy Babylon the Great? (18:10, 17, 19)

Who gathered together to make war against Him who sat on the white horse? (19:19)

Besides the books that contained records of works done, what other book was opened? (20:12)

Who or what is the Lamb's bride/wife? (21:2, 9–10)

Who is speaking in 22:12–16?

A NOTE FROM YOUR BIBLE STUDY MENTOR

You did it! You completed this Bible study course and now have a fundamental knowledge of the Bible.

As any Bible teacher will say, there is still much to learn. Understanding the Bible is a lifelong process. However, each time you read a portion of it, you will learn something new about God, His Son, the Holy Spirit and you. At the same time, you will feed your soul and spirit.

Sheriena McEvers attended Trinity Bible Institute in North Dakota.

This workbook is a result of putting her online Bible study in print
which can be found at www.simplebiblelessons.com.

She and her husband live in Nebraska. They have two sons and two grandchildren.

Find out more about Sheriena at www.sherienamcevers.com

www.ingramcontent.com/pod-product-compliance
Lightning Source LLC
La Vergne TN
LVHW061331060426
835512LV00013B/2600